KNOWN
a year of questions

KNOWN
a year of questions

Curt Wilkinson, PhD

blueparkbooks

blueparkbooks
www.blueparkbooks.com

Publisher's Cataloging-in-Publication P-CIP Data

Wilkinson, Curt (Curtis A.)

    Known: A Year of Questions / Curt Wilkinson
    p. cm.

Summary: A year-long book of days presenting engaging questions that help deepen relationships and develop a greater understanding of self.

ISBN: 978-1-7337250-4-0

Library of Congress Control Number: 2021913831

1. Relationships   2. Marriage   3. Identity
4. Personal Growth   5. Book of Days

I. Title: KNOWN
II. Title: A Year of Questions

Non-fiction | Paperback

Printed in the United States of America

For Karl

"JUDGE A MAN BY HIS QUESTIONS
RATHER THAN HIS ANSWERS."

—Voltaire

CONTENTS

HOW TO USE THIS BOOK
Pages 27 -32

JANUARY

F E B R U A R Y

MARCH

APRIL

MAY

JUNE

JULY

AUGUST

SEPTEMBER

OCTOBER

NOVEMBER

DECEMBER

"I NEVER LEARN ANYTHING TALKING.
I ONLY LEARN THINGS WHEN I ASK QUESTIONS."

—Lou Holtz

HOW TO USE
THIS BOOK

Back before married life, before kids, I had a roommate named Karl. We lived in a small, thrift store-appointed apartment in a suburb just outside Chicago. Karl had recently moved from Minneapolis to start a new job, but his closest friends were still living up north. "What would you think about taking a road trip this weekend?" Karl asked. "Do you want to drive up to Minneapolis?"

Now, I had always thought of myself as a guy who was up for anything, but this idea seemed absurd. Why would anyone spend almost half of their precious weekend driving? "Karl, what are we going to do stuck in your car for 16 hours?" He smiled, and without giving it a thought, he said, "We can talk."

That weekend, Karl became one of my best friends. Today, more than 30 years later, we're still great friends, and I think it's safe to say, we know each other well.

WHY I WROTE THIS BOOK

One of the reasons Karl is such a close friend is because he has learned the power of asking great questions. I'm privileged to have a friend who is not afraid to explore all the "whats" and "whys" of life. No topic is off limits in our friendship, and I'm convinced that our transparency brings us together. Being vulnerable and sharing life together is a big part of what it means to be human. It's what motivated me to write this book.

> WE LONG TO BE
> DEEPLY KNOWN
> AND, IN SPITE OF IT,
> TO FIND OURSELVES
> STILL DEEPLY LOVED.

I am concerned there are far too many pixels between us. We're missing out on the deep stuff, the messy stuff, the stuff that defines what it means to be known. My desire for you is that you might be truly known and loved, and that you would truly know and love others.

This journey of knowing and being known requires time. It comes by doing life together, struggling together, and when the moment is right, by asking thoughtful questions that flesh out our fears, our motives, and our dreams.

My hope is that this book will help you grow—that you might go deeper with others and come to a better understanding of yourself. I have chosen a topic for each day of the year, followed by some great quotes* and suggested questions.

*The quotes in this book do not always reflect my personal thoughts or opinions. In many cases I intentionally selected a quote to raise an issue or encourage debate.

I realize that all my questions may not resonate with you. Please don't let a lame question hang you up. Each topic is an invitation to have a conversation—a chance to explore what it means to be known.

My hope is that you'll see this book as a journey—one that you can choose to take by yourself, or share with someone you love. I encourage you to come up with questions of your own. You might even consider using this book as a daily journal, writing down your own questions in the margins as you go.

As I was writing this book I made a discovery. I was surprised to find that almost all of my questions are, at their core, a modified expression of three fundamental questions:

1. How are you responding to your PAST?
2. How content are you with your PRESENT?
3. How are you pursuing your FUTURE?

Our answers to these three core questions reveal who we are in profound ways. I challenge you to answer them for yourself in the process of posing them to others. I also challenge you to develop the skill of formulating follow up questions based on the answers you receive to the questions you ask. Real knowing and deep relationships only come when we push past the surface and ask questions that go deeper.

The calendar format of this book was never intended to restrict or require. For some, it may be more helpful to flip through these pages and pursue only the topics that interest you. The benefit of the calendar is that it gives you a reason to connect every day. I hope, too, that by following the dates, you will be challenged to pursue some topics you might otherwise miss or avoid.

IS THIS BOOK FOR YOU?

I wrote this book because I believe a well-thought-out, and carefully worded question is one of the most loving acts of kindness you could ever give to another human being. Questions are my "love language." I wrote this book because I want to know my wife better and I want to know my children and my friends better too. Here are four ways I believe this book might be helpful for you.

Relationship Building

First, and foremost, this book was written for people who want to cultivate deep and meaningful relationships. It's an easy and accessible way for spouses, families, friends, and co-workers to connect every day of the year. The entries are short, the topics are predetermined, and the questions will get a conversation started. This book was designed to be a simple and meaningful way to grow closer to the ones who matter most in your life.

Self-Awareness / Identity

Secondly, this book was created as a resource for personal growth. I'm hoping you might use this book to supplement your quiet times or morning meditation. The topic of each day will help you pursue a greater understanding of who you are.

Team Building

Some of the questions in this book
may be far too personal for the office,
but in the hands of a good facilitator,
these topics can be used to "break
the ice" and build trust on your team.
One way is to start a meeting with
a few questions based on the topic
of the day.

Character Development / Fiction Writers

Finally, this book represents a great
resource for fiction writers. It can be
challenging to come up with fresh
characters for your next novel. These
characters need to have a "spine"
that motivates their every move;
they need to be unique. These questions
can help bring your characters to life.

TIPS FOR THE RELUCTANT

In writing this book and sharing my idea with others, I
quickly realized that not everyone is eager to spend an
evening asking and answering deep questions. If this
describes you or someone you love, please consider
these simple suggestions:

1. Choose a time when you both can "lean in."

2. Don't feel pressure to answer all the questions.

3. YES/NO answers may need to be enough.

4. Modify questions so they apply to you.

5. Remember to protect one another's answers.

6. Ask permission to pursue the "why" behind the "what."

7. Make your follow up questions encouraging.

VULNERABILITY

Finally, to be known, and to be loved requires vulnerability. Yes, it means taking a risk, but I hope it's one you'll be willing to take. Be warned, KNOWN is a book filled with lots of delicate and personal questions. It was difficult to choose 366 of life's topics and issues without leaving out something important. I realize I may have not included some topics and questions that are important to you. I would like to think that if I had the opportunity to drive from Chicago to Minneapolis with you, I might have the opportunity to ask additional questions—ones meant just for you. So, please don't use the questions in this book to divide, and separate us. I believe questions are best used for learning to understand, to appreciate, and acknowledge. My deepest desire is to be known and to be loved in spite of all I am. I pray that you might be known this way too, and that this book will help you on your way!

Curt Wilkinson, June 2021

PS: As you can tell from this book, my life is filled with questions, but I'd like to think I've also found some really great answers. Some are worth sharing. If you're curious, please visit me at: curtwilkinson.com

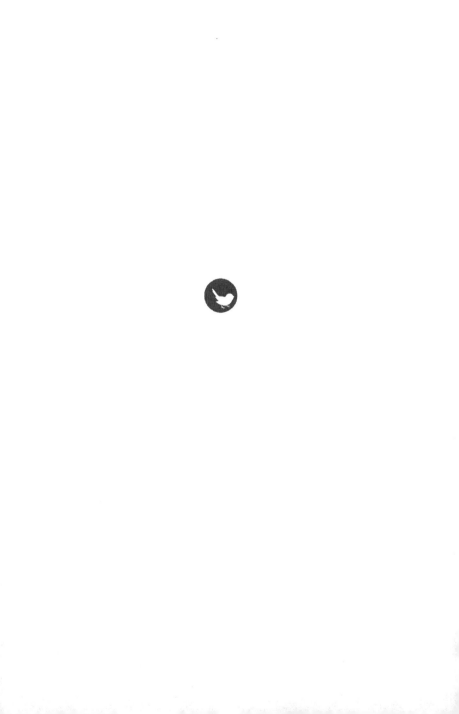

A NEW YEAR

"We will open the book. Its pages are blank. We are going to put words on them ourselves. The book is called Opportunity and its first chapter is New Year's Day."

—Edith Lovejoy Pierce

"There is nothing magical about the flip of the calendar, but it represents a clean break, a new hope, and a blank canvas."

—Jason Soroski

Happy New Year! Welcome to KNOWN: A YEAR OF QUESTIONS. New Year's Day is a chance to hit the reset button, to clean the slate, and to begin again.

Do you believe in making New Year's resolutions?

If you could accomplish one goal this year, what would it be?

Do you have any New Year's Day rituals?

Is there one New Year's Day in your life that is especially memorable?

What's one thing from last year you're glad to be leaving behind?

What's one thing from last year you want to keep doing this year?

Other than being one year older, how do you think your life will be different one year from now?

Are you ready to spend the year asking some very important questions?

ACCIDENTS

"You'll learn more from your accidents than anything that you could ever learn at school."
—Billy Joel

"They're funny things, Accidents. You never have them till you're having them."
—A. A. Milne

Accidents remind us that life is not always under control. Some accidents are small, like spilling your milk; but others carry enduring guilt, those fatal mistakes that ruin lives.

How did your parents respond to small accidents, like spilling your milk, wetting the bed, or breaking a plate?

How do you respond when someone is careless and their accidental mistake affects you?

Is there someone you need to forgive for an accident that affected you?

Do you know someone who is obsessed with safety and consumed with avoiding accidents?

How does someone cope with the guilt and pain that comes from accidentally hurting someone?

What's the worst accident you were responsible for?

Do you forgive yourself for your own accidents?

Does the possibility of an accident keep you from taking risks and pursuing adventure?

ADDICTION

"First you take a drink, then the drink takes a drink, then the drink takes you."

—F. Scott Fitzgerald

"If you can quit for a day, you can quit for a lifetime."

—Benjamin Alire Sáenz

The demon of addiction ruins lives. At the start, it brings relief, but it's a relief that requires your soul to sustain. One day, you find your addiction is causing more pain than the pain you were trying to escape.

Do you think addiction is a disease or a genetic disposition?

Have you observed serious addiction firsthand?

Do you think there are innocent addictions, like chocolate?

If you were to be tempted by addiction, what substance or habit would be your downfall?

Have you ever had to confront somebody about their addictive behavior?

What do you think are the signs someone has gone from being a person who enjoys something to a person who needs something?

Have you ever consumed a pint of ice cream or a whole pizza to make yourself feel better?

Would you be willing to organize an intervention if you discovered someone had an addiction out of control?

ADOPTION

"Not flesh of my flesh, nor bone of my bone, but still miraculously my own. Never forget for a single minute, you didn't grow under my heart but in it."

—Fleur Conkling Heyliger

"Adoption was a bumpy ride—very bumpy. But God, was it worth the fight."

—Mariska Hargitay

Adoption is both noble and divine, but just as in childbirth, it doesn't come without pain and struggle. The labor of childbirth requires hours; the labor of adoption requires a lifetime.

Do you know someone who was adopted?

If you were adopted, would you want to connect at some point with your biological parents?

Do you believe siblings should be required to be adopted into the same family?

Have you ever visited an orphanage?

What are your thoughts on international adoption or interracial adoption?

When do you feel a child should be told they were adopted?

Do you believe an adopted child should be given a new name?

Are you open to adopting a child?

AIRPLANES

"I'm flying! I'm flying! I'm flying in the sky!"

—Aly Wilkinson (first flight, age three)

"Sometimes, flying feels too God-like to be attained by man. Sometimes, the world from above seems too beautiful, too wonderful, too distant for human eyes to see."

—Charles Lindbergh

A 747 passenger plane weighs over 400,000 pounds, and can take flight in less than 30 seconds. A flight from Los Angeles to Tokyo takes less than 12 hours. Airplanes are the closest thing mere mortals have to overcoming time and space.

When did you take your first flight in an airplane?

Does flying make you nervous?

Do you have a "flight from hell" story?

Do you know anyone who survived a plane crash?

Would you ever consider getting your pilot's license?

Window seat or aisle?

Have you ever flown first class?

Where would you go if you could fly anywhere in the world?

Would you appreciate being surprised by someone you love if they said, "Pack your bags, we're flying to Hawaii in three hours!"?

ALCOHOL

"Here's to alcohol: the cause of, and answer to, all of life's problems."
—Matt Groenig

"Beer is made by men, wine by God."
—Martin Luther

Alcohol is a topic that can produce passionate discussion and debate. Perhaps there is benefit in making a distinction between drinking and getting drunk, between appreciation and abuse.

Was alcohol present in your family growing up?

When was the first time you were offered alcohol?

What is your response when the medical survey asks you how many alcoholic beverages you consume a week?

Have you ever had to take someone's keys to keep them from driving while under the influence?

What level of appreciation do you have for the craft of making fine wine, beer, and other alcoholic beverages?

Was drinking a big part of your college experience?

Do you think 21 is the appropriate age to legally consume alcohol?

How do you think children should be taught about alcohol?

Do you ever worry that the drinking habits of someone you love are getting out of control?

ALL-NIGHTERS

"Love is staying up all night with a sick child, or a healthy adult."

—David Frost

"Staying up all night is a waste of sleeping, and a waste of sleeping is a waste of dreaming, and dreaming is important because the more dreams you have, the better chance you have of one coming true."

—Izzie Reeves

An "all-nighter" is the practice of staying up all night to finish a task. Your first "all-nighter" is usually the result of foolish procrastination combined with a deadline clearly posted in a college course syllabus.

Have you ever stayed up all night to finish a task?

Is the "all-nighter" a common practice in your life?

When was the last time you stayed up all night for something?

What was the longest night of your life?

Having you ever stayed up all night because you were in love, inspired, or just having a blast?

Do you think less of people who procrastinate or wait for inspiration before beginning a project?

Have you ever had to stay up all night with someone because they were sick or going through a crisis?

Can you think of a good reason to stay up all night tonight?

ANGER

"You can tell the greatness of a man by what makes him angry."

—Abraham Lincoln

"Where there is anger, there is always pain underneath."

—Eckhart Tolle

Find the things that make you angry. These are the things that matter, the things you were born to make right. Is it chaos? Injustice? Cheating? Lying? Take your anger and use it for good.

What makes you angry?

How did your parents express their anger?

How do you express your anger?

At what moment did you find yourself the most angry you have ever been?

Is there something or someone in your life that has caused you to be angry for a long time?

Do you count to ten when you're angry?

Have you ever felt righteous anger toward something evil in the world?

How can you do a better job controlling your anger this coming year?

ANNIVERSARIES

"Remember to celebrate milestones as you prepare for the road ahead."

—*Nelson Mandela*

"A wedding anniversary is the celebration of love, trust, partnership, tolerance, and tenacity. The order varies for any given year."

—*Paul Sweeney*

Time is a precious thing. It's a commodity we can't control, we can't get back, and we can't buy more of. What we can do is celebrate its significance.

What anniversaries do you celebrate?

Do you remember what your parents did to celebrate their wedding anniversary?

What's the longest anyone in your family has been married?

Do you remember the anniversary of hard things in your life, like the passing of a loved one?

If you were to create your own annual holiday, what would it be and which day would you celebrate it?

What is the biggest, most lavish anniversary celebration you've ever been to?

Do you think anniversaries are overrated?

Do you think couples should renew their wedding vows?

How would you like to celebrate life's most significant anniversaries?

ANNOYANCES

"Be happy. It really annoys negative people."

—Ricky Gervais

"I like long walks, especially when they are taken by people who annoy me."

—Noel Coward

It's not hard to be annoying—just chew with your mouth open or constantly change lanes when driving. Learning not to get annoyed? Now that's impressive.

What are some things that annoy you?

Have you ever purposefully tried to annoy someone?

How do you respond when a kid kicks the back of your seat at the theater?

Is there someone from your childhood who made it their purpose in life to annoy you?

Is there someone you know so well that you know exactly how to "push their buttons"?

What's one thing you find yourself doing over and over again that might be annoying?

Do you ever annoy yourself?

What are some things you have done to ignore an annoyance?

Why do you think some people are so easily annoyed?

ANTAGONISTS

"He that struggles with us strengthens our nerves and sharpens our skill. Our antagonist is our helper."

—Edmund Burke

"You don't really understand an antagonist until you understand why he's a protagonist in his own version of the world."

—John Rogers

There's always a bad guy in the story. In fact, without the antagonist, there's no reason for a hero. Unfortunately, the villains in our life don't always bring out our best.

Who are some of your favorite antagonists in books and movies?

What do you think are the qualities of a great bad guy?

Have you ever felt that there was someone in your life who was pursuing your demise?

Do you feel there was ever a time when you played the role of antagonist in someone's life?

How do circumstances, frustrations, and other obstacles function as antagonists in your life?

They say a good villain always preys on the weakness of the hero. How would a villain get to yours?

Do you think that fiction makes too much of villains, that really the only obstacle in life is ourself?

Have you ever rescued someone from the "bad guy"?

ARGUMENTS

"Don't worry when I argue with you; worry when I stop because it means there's nothing left to fight for."

—Anonymous

"Raise your words, not your voice. It is rain that grows flowers, not thunder."

—Rumi

Arguments are often more about our need to be right than our need to be reconciled. There are civil ways to argue, and it never hurts to consider the possibility we might be wrong.

Do you like to argue?

Even if you don't like to argue, are you good at making an argument?

Did you remember your parents spending a lot of time arguing?

Do you have friends or family members who just aren't happy unless they're engaged in an argument?

What was your last big argument about?

Have you ever had a big argument about a small or petty thing?

How do you diffuse the emotion from a heated argument?

What issues or topics tend to lead you toward controversy and heated arguments?

AROMAS

"For the sense of smell, almost more than any other, has the power to recall memories, and it's a pity we use it so little."

—Rachel Carson

"A book has got a smell. A new book smells great. An old book smells even better. An old book smells like ancient Egypt."

—Ray Bradbury

There's nothing like the sense of smell to bring us back to our past. Photographs can help us remember life's moments, but aromas help us relive them.

Do you have a connection between certain smells and certain memories?

Is there an aroma from someone cooking that brings you back to a favorite meal or moment?

Have you ever lost your sense of smell?

Are there any scents or smells that you find repulsive?

Is there fragrance from nature that makes you smile, like the ocean, the forest, or field of wild flowers?

Do you intentionally set out to fill your home, your car, or your office with a special fragrance?

Is there a perfume or cologne that you associate with someone special?

Are there smells that you associate with spring, summer, winter, or fall?

ART

"Art enables us to find ourselves and lose ourselves at the same time."

—*Thomas Merton*

"Every child is an artist. The problem is how to remain an artist once we grow up."

—*Pablo Picasso*

People have been struggling to answer the question "What is art?" for centuries. One of the reasons for this is that art affects us all on a deeply personal level. That is why we love it.

———————————————

Are you an art lover?

Would you consider yourself to be an artist or artistic?

Do have a particular art form or medium that is especially interesting to you?

What do you think of modern art?

Do you like to visit art museums and art galleries when you travel to different cities?

Do you have a favorite artist?

Are any of your friends or family members trying to make a living as an artist or in the art industry?

At what point do you feel a starving artist should give up their dream?

Have you ever considered buying a piece of original artwork?

RACISM

"No one is born hating another person because of the color of his skin, or his background, or his religion. People must learn to hate, and if they can learn to hate, they can be taught to love, for love comes more naturally to the human heart than its opposite."

—Nelson Mandela

"In a racist society, it is not enough to be non-racist. We must be anti-racist."

—Angela Davis

Today we stop to reflect on the life and work of Dr. Martin Luther King, Jr. Unfortunately, the freedom and ideals he stood for are still far from reality.

Have you ever been the victim of prejudice or racism?

Is this a topic you find difficult or unsafe to talk about?

What books or films do you feel have revealed the truth and realities surrounding racism in this country?

Have you found it difficult to consider the areas in your life where you might hold some prejudice?

Who do you believe are some modern-day heroes in the fight against racism?

Do you have friends who are of a different race than you?

What would you say is the number one thing we could be doing to end racism?

What's one thing that you've observed in the world that gives you hope regarding this issue?

ASKING QUESTIONS

"The wise man doesn't give the right answers; he poses the right questions."

—Claude Lévi-Strauss

"I believe people who love us help give us answers and not more questions. They show us how to do something; they don't ask us how we are going to do something."

—David DeNotaris

This entire book was designed to show the value of asking good questions, but questions are only the beginning. It's through our answers that we reveal who we really are.

Would you consider yourself a curious person?

Does the art of conversation come easy to you?

What's a question you wish someone would ask you?

How can someone go about earning the right to ask deep and personal questions?

Is there a topic of conversation that you consider "off-limits"?

What's the longest conversation you've ever had in your life?

Does answering a personal question require the asker reciprocate by answering the question too?

Do you usually answer yes/no questions with a "yes" or "no," or do you expound with the reasons behind your answer?

Are you tired of answering all these questions?

AUNTS & UNCLES

"A man with a hump-backed uncle mustn't make fun of another man's cross-eyed aunt."

—*Mark Twain*

"The best aunts and uncles are not substitute parents; they are co-conspirators."

—*Unknown*

Aunts and uncles reveal so much about our parents. They're siblings, from the same family, but represent a unique variation on the theme.

Do you have aunts and uncles?

Are you an aunt or uncle?

How would you describe the perfect aunt or uncle?

Are you especially close to one of your aunts or uncles?

Would you describe one of your aunts or uncles as the "odd one" or "black sheep" of the family?

Where do your parents fall in the birth order of their families?

Do your aunts and uncles live close to you, or are they spread out all over?

Do your aunts and uncles send you birthday and Christmas presents?

Do you have a close relationship with your siblings that makes you want to be a good aunt or uncle?

AUTHORITY

"I fought the law and the law won."

—Sonny Curtis

"Authority without wisdom is like a heavy axe without an edge, fitter to bruise than polish."

—Anne Bradstreet

Authority that is loving and kind produces a safe context where life can flourish. Authority that is corrupt causes the soul of society to decay.

When you hear the word *authority*, does it conjure up positive or negative thoughts?

Was there a period in your life when you struggled with authority?

How did your parents model the role of authority in your life?

Was there a person, school, or institution that abused their authority over you?

Is there someone currently in authority who you believe is using their power wisely?

Are you someone who pursues positions of power and authority?

How can we change the expression of authority from one of power to one of wisdom, knowledge, and expertise?

What are some ways we can hold those in authority accountable for their actions?

AWKWARD MOMENTS

"If you're in an awkward position, feel comfortable enough to walk away."

—*Beau Mirchoff*

"I don't have awkward moments. I have an awkward life, occasionally interrupted by normalcy."

—*Robert Pattinson*

We all have moments in life when we wish we could disappear. We can conceal our flaws, but inevitably, they come out at the perfectly wrong time.

What are some of life's most awkward moments?

Did you go through an awkward stage growing up?

Was there ever an awkward wardrobe moment, when you wore something and later wondered what you were thinking?

What was your most awkward moment on a date?

Have you ever destroyed or deleted photographs to hide an awkward moment?

What do you do when you find yourself in the middle of someone else's awkward moment?

Do you have a "caught with my hand in the cookie jar" story?

Is there someone you know who seems to have more than their fair share of awkward moments?

How do you respond to an awkward moment?

BAD PURCHASES

"When I shop, the world gets better, and the world is better, but then it's not, and I need to do it again."

—Rebecca Bloomwood

"Good decisions come from experience. Experience comes from making bad decisions."

—Mark Twain

We've all purchased that thing we had to have only to find ourselves deceived and disappointed. *Caveat emptor* is Latin for "buyer beware" and proves that making a bad purchase is nothing new.

Are you an easy target for a pushy salesperson?

What products are the most tempting for you?

What's the most money you've ever spent on an impulse purchase?

Are your parents people who make wise purchases?

What's the worst purchase you've ever made?

How intense or comprehensive is your research when making an important purchase?

Have you ever had to persuade someone to buy something?

How do you feel about returning items that don't fully meet your expectations?

BEDTIME STORIES

"I will defend the importance of bedtime stories to my last gasp."

—*J. K. Rowling*

"Obsessed by a fairy tale, we spend our lives searching for a magic door and a lost kingdom of peace."

—*Eugene O'Neill*

Somewhere between "Once upon a time" and "They lived happily ever after" we learned to imagine a life filled with magic, mystery, romance, and wonder.

Do you have a favorite children's book?

Did your family read storybooks aloud before bed?

Do you still own books from your childhood?

Was there a character in a children's book that proved to be your favorite, like Winnie the Pooh?

Do you like books that rhyme?

When you read aloud, do you use different voices for each character?

Was there a scene, character, or situation in a storybook that gave you bad dreams?

What is the value of reading books to children?

How have books from your childhood influenced your dreams and imagination?

BEING ALONE

"What a lovely surprise to finally discover how unlonely being alone can be."

—Ellen Burstyn

"Loneliness expresses the pain of being alone, and solitude expresses the glory of being alone."

—Paul Tillich

There's a big difference between being alone and feeling alone. How wonderful to be alone, confident that in your heart you're surrounded by those who love you.

———————————————

Do you enjoy being alone?

Was your childhood filled with solitude and time to yourself, or were you always surrounded by others?

Was there a time in your life when you felt especially alone?

Is there a place you like to go specifically to be alone?

Do you have trouble eating alone at a restaurant?

When you're alone, do you like to fill the silence with music or the background noise of a coffee shop or park?

Were you ever sent to your room or forced to be alone as punishment?

What is the best thing that has come as a result of you spending time alone or taking a personal retreat?

BEING FAMOUS

"We are taught these days that being famous is more important than actually doing something."

—Ben Howard

"When you're poor, you are invisible. Every poor person will tell you nobody sees you. So being famous was me just wanting to be seen."

—Viola Davis

Culture has somehow convinced us that public praise for the superficial is far better than living an anonymous life of meaning and substance.

Do you ever wish you were famous?

Why do you think fame ruins so many lives?

Who are some people who have handled their fame wisely and still seem to live a normal, balanced life?

What do you think Andy Warhol meant when he said people get "15 minutes of fame"?

Do you think it's okay for parents to push their children into the limelight?

If you could be famous for one thing, what would it be?

Do you think that social media produces in us a stronger desire to be famous?

Is it possible to avoid the pitfalls of fame and still be the best at something?

BEING RICH

"There is a gigantic difference between earning a great deal of money and being rich."

—Marlene Dietrich

"I don't care what anyone says, being rich is a good thing."

—Mark Cuban

We try to convince ourselves that being rich is just a mindset, but I'm not sure we're buying it. Money enables you to solve problems and make life better.

Are you content in your current financial situation?

As a child, did you see your family as poor, rich, or somewhere in between?

If you're not currently content with your money situation, how much more would you need to get there?

Do you believe money can't buy happiness?

Are you intentionally setting money aside every month to invest and prepare for the future?

Would you be content to continue working your whole life, or are you working toward being financially independent?

Is there something extravagant you would buy if you were rich?

What good is it if someone gains all the money in the world only to wind up losing their soul in the process?

Is pursuing contentment wiser than pursuing wealth?

JANUARY 25

BEING SICK

"Health is not valued till sickness comes."

—*Thomas Fuller*

"Your illness does not define you. Your strength and courage does."

—*Anonymous*

A sickness that can be cured is a nuisance, but the incurable disease strips away hope. That's when we turn to alternative treatments, miracles, and prayer.

———————————————

Would you consider yourself to be healthy?

Were you often sick as a child?

What's the most serious bout with sickness you've ever had?

Do you like to be left alone when you're sick, or do you prefer to have someone tending to you and nursing you back to health?

Are you difficult to be around when you're sick?

Have you had to walk through a terminal illness with a friend or family member?

Have you ever had a pain, condition, or illness that could not be diagnosed?

Are there diseases or health conditions that run in your family?

What is your opinion about alternative forms of medicine or homeopathic solutions?

BEST ADVICE

"Advice is what we ask for when we already know the answer but wish we didn't."

—Erica Jong

"Advice is like snow, the softer it falls, the longer it dwells upon, and the deeper it sinks into the mind."

—Samuel Taylor Coleridge

Here's some advice on giving and accepting advice: Be slow to accept it and even slower to give it. The best advice comes from people who are vulnerable enough to share their mistakes so you don't make them too.

———————————————

Why is it so easy to give advice?

What is the best advice that you've ever been given?

Is there someone in your life who consistently proves to be the voice of wisdom?

What's the worst advice you've ever been given?

Do you feel especially equipped to give advice on a specific issue or topic?

Is there a book, website, or resource that you go to when you're looking for advice or wisdom?

If you could get advice from anyone, living or dead, who would it be?

Have you ever asked for advice when you already knew the right thing to do?

BEST DAY EVER

"The two most important days of your life are the day you are born and the day you find out why."

—Unknown

"The best day in your life is the one on which you decide your life is your own. It is an amazing journey, and you alone are responsible for the quality of it. This is the day your life really begins."

—Unknown

It's the combination of where you are, who you're with, what you're doing, and how you feel. When all those things are the best they can be, you're living the best day ever.

Do you have a "best day ever"?

What's one of the best days from your childhood?

What was the best day you've had in the past year?

If you had the power to live a day where you could do anything or be anywhere with anyone, what would you do?

Have you ever tried to create someone else's best day ever?

Do you journal your days so you don't forget them?

If you could ask anyone, living or dead, about their best day ever, who would you ask?

Could you have a "best day ever" without big budgets, exotic locations, and expensive toys?

What could you do today to make this a best day ever?

BEST FRIENDS

"A real friend is one who walks in when the rest of the world walks out."

—Walter Winchell

"There is nothing on this earth more to be prized than true friendship."

—Thomas Aquinas

Friends are better than money in the bank. They give you someone to share your life with, and the more you share, the richer your life becomes.

Are you a good friend?

Who were some of your best friends from childhood?

Who would you consider to be your closest friends right now?

What's the difference between a friend and an acquaintance?

Do you feel like it's possible to be good friends with someone you've never met in person?

What is the foundation of a good friendship?

Is there a friendship you've lost and miss?

What's the longest friendship you've had?

What's one thing you can do to be a better friend?

BEST QUEST

"You never know how a good quest is going to end."

—Elizabeth Gilbert

"The greatest quest in life is to reach one's potential."

—Mychal Wynn

A quest is a long and arduous search for something important. Life is a quest, but instead of looking for the Holy Grail, we're looking for purpose and meaning.

Do you like books and movies with a quest theme?

What do you think is the greatest quest story of all time?

How is your life like a quest?

Is there something physical or tangible that you have been seeking for a long, long time?

Do you envy people who have a tangible quest, like curing cancer, as the focus of their life?

How do you think having a quest affects how we live and how long we live?

What would be something you could pursue with passion for the rest of your life?

What gives your life purpose and meaning right now, and how does it keep you looking forward to tomorrow?

BEST SCHOOL SUBJECTS

"History was my favorite subject in school; it was the only subject I excelled in. I love the idea of history and the idea that we may have the opportunity to learn from our past mistakes."

—Cary Elwes

"Dear Math, I'm sick and tired of finding your "x." Just accept the fact that she is gone. Move on, dude."

—Unknown

Our love for school may have been affected by how we were treated in the halls or playground, but for many of us, it had a lot to do with our success in the classroom.

Did/do you like school?

What was the first school subject that made you feel like you had potential?

Were you traumatized by reading aloud, spelling bees, or going to the chalkboard?

Was there a teacher or professor who turned a boring or difficult subject into something you love?

If you could teach one class on any subject, what would it be?

What's one class or subject that you felt was a waste of time?

How can our current education system be changed to more effectively engage learners?

What are your thoughts about online learning?

JANUARY 31

BEST TEACHER

"The mediocre teacher tells. The good teacher explains. The superior teacher demonstrates. The great teacher inspires."

—William Arthur Ward

"I have come to believe that a great teacher is a great artist and that there are as few as there are any other great artists. Teaching might even be the greatest of the arts since the medium is the human mind and spirit."

—John Steinbeck

Other than our parents, there are few people who have more influence over what we love and who we become than the school teachers of our youth.

Who was your favorite teacher?

Is there a teaching technique, lab, or field trip that you will never forget?

Is there a classroom that you can still visualize in your mind?

Who was the most eccentric teacher you've ever had?

What did teachers do to make you love the subject they taught?

Have you ever considered becoming a teacher?

Have you ever contacted or visited a teacher to thank them for how they impacted your life?

What would happen if we paid teachers as much as we pay lawyers and doctors?

How can we teach teachers to teach better?

BETRAYAL

"Et tu, Brute?"

—Julius Caesar (William Shakespeare)

"It is easier to forgive an enemy than to forgive a friend."

—William Blake

Life is hard, so we might expect some people to be mean. But when the ones we love and trust most, prove to be disloyal, we are devastated.

Have you ever been betrayed?

Are you guilty of betraying another's trust?

What would it take to recover from the betrayal of a close friend or family member?

Do you have any favorite stories, books, or movies that are based on betrayal, revenge, and forgiveness?

What do you believe was the most profound act of betrayal of all time?

Do you think that everyone has a breaking point where their own self-preservation comes first?

Is there someone you disdain for the way they have betrayed a friend or family member?

Are there relationships in your life that need to be redeemed or restored after a betrayal?

Do you believe that the effects of betrayal are irreversible?

FOUR SEASONS

"The seasons are what a symphony ought to be—four perfect movements in harmony with each other."

—Arthur Rubenstein

"To be interested in the changing seasons is a happier state of mind than to be hopelessly in love with spring."

—George Santayana

It's Groundhog Day, and for those of us who grew up experiencing clear transitions of spring to summer to fall to winter, the changing of the four seasons holds deep significance. It's how we mark the passing of time.

Did you grow up in a place with four distinct seasons?

What are your favorite and least favorite seasons?

Would you ever be open to moving to a different climate with different seasons?

In the north, people are always dreaming of a "white" Christmas. What do people in the tropics dream of?

Is there something for you that marks the beginning of a new season, like baseball's opening day, the first blossom, or first snow?

Did the groundhog see its shadow this year?

When are you most aware a season is changing? Is it the date? The weather? The marketing campaigns?

Are there some moments when the seasons turn that are filled with memories and nostalgia?

BINGES

"I binge when I'm happy. When everything is going really well, every day is like I'm at a birthday party."
—Kirstie Alley

"I think the main reason that people binge watch is because they can. We're like dogs, really. If we like something, we tend to gorge ourselves on it until there's no more left."
—D.B. Weiss

Nothing brings more significance to the word *binge* **than Netflix. You can watch a whole TV season in one weekend, which feels like the accomplishment of running a marathon, but without all the sweat.**

Are you prone to binge?

In what activities are you most likely to excessively indulge?

What is your personal record for your longest continuous binge?

Have you ever had to confront someone on their binge behavior?

What's your food binge of choice?

Do you think we live in a culture that has legitimized bingeing as a coping mechanism?

Do you feel ashamed after a long binge?

What's the possibility of finding something to binge on that's good for us, like healthy eating or learning something new?

BIRTHDAYS

"I don't mind getting older; it's a privilege denied to so many!"

—Chris Geiger

"The more you praise and celebrate your life, the more there is in life to celebrate."

—Oprah Winfrey

Birthdays are personal things. Some people like to be surprised, others like big parties, and still others want to celebrate in quieter ways. Regardless, it's a great feeling to know people are excited you were born.

How old are you going to be this year?

How did your family celebrate birthdays when you were growing up?

Do you have a favorite birthday memory?

Are you a big party person, or do you prefer something smaller and more personal?

What's your favorite birthday cake?

Is there one birthday present that you will always remember?

Do you like to plan birthday parties for your friends and family?

Is there something special you'd like to do for your birthday next year?

BODILY FUNCTIONS

"I burp, I fart. I'm a real woman."

—Kate Winslet

"Beans, beans the musical fruit. The more you eat the more you toot."

—Unknown

Our bodies can't be trusted. We think we've got things under control and then, without permission, our bodies decide to humiliate us at the most inopportune times.

Is this a topic you feel comfortable talking about?

How did your family handle the inevitable expressions of the sounds and smells of life?

Did you grow up using family friendly words for bodily functions?

What was your most embarrassing moment when it comes to bodily functions?

Did you have a "nightmare nausea" story?

Who is the most shameless person you've ever met in regard to bodily functions?

Have you ever participated in a belching contest?

What's the longest time you've ever spent in the bathroom trying to recover from a bout with your body?

Do you stock your bathroom with air fresheners, candles, and matches?

BOLDNESS

"Freedom lies in being bold."

—Robert Frost

"People who ask confidently get more than those who are hesitant and uncertain. When you've figured out what you want to ask for, do it with certainty, boldness, and confidence."

—Jack Canfield

Boldness is one of those qualities that seems to have a good side and a bad side. To be bold in battle is to be courageous and brave, but to be bold in fashion may have people laughing behind your back.

What do you think it means to be bold?

Would you consider yourself to be a bold person?

What is the boldest decision you've ever made?

Is there someone you know who is bold in a bad way?

What causes boldness to cross the line from being a good trait to a bad one?

In what area of life could you be less timid and boldly take more risks?

Do you think that men and women think about boldness in different ways?

Have you ever seen someone's decision to be bold and assertive backfire?

Who is someone whose boldness you admire?

BUCKET LIST

"One day, you will wake up and there won't be any more time to do the things you've always wanted. Do it now."

—Paulo Coelho

"Twenty years from now you will be more disappointed by the things you didn't do than by the ones you did do. So throw off the bowlines. Sail away from the safe harbor. Catch the trade winds in your sails. Explore. Dream. Discover."

—Mark Twain

A bucket list forces us to consider all the things that life has to offer. For some, it's adventure and adrenaline; for others it's beauty and wonder. A bucket list shows you what you think is important.

Do you have a bucket list?

Do you think bucket lists are just for old people who feel like they are running out of time?

What is the most important thing you want to do before you die?

Does your bucket list require you to have lots of money?

What's the most amazing thing you've ever heard of or considered doing before you die?

Do you think bucket lists change as you get older?

Is a bucket list something you create yourself, or is it something to create and do with someone you love?

What are five things you would put on your bucket list if you had to make one today?

BUDGETING

"A budget is telling your money where to go instead of wondering where it went."

—Dave Ramsey

"A budget takes the fun out of money."

—Mason Cooley

If you're fortunate to have enough money left over at the end of the month, budgeting can be fun. But when money is tight and you're trying to stretch every penny, a budget can feel like a noose around your neck.

Do you have a budget that you stick to?

What would you say to the person who believes budgeting is only for those who don't have money left over at the end of the month?

Is there money that you set aside every paycheck for something special, like a vacation?

Do you budget money to replace items that wear out, like a car or a roof?

Do you have a retirement strategy?

Do you believe in donating money to charities, churches, and other non-profit organizations?

Do you know what your first, second, and third biggest expenses are every month?

Do you use a special software or spreadsheet to organize your finances, bills, and budget?

BULLIES

"If you have to hurt other people in order to feel powerful, you are an extremely weak individual."
—Bobby J. Mattingly

"Never be bullied into silence. Never allow yourself to be made a victim. Accept no one's definition of your life; define yourself."
—Robert Frost

Current estimates suggest that nearly 30% of all adolescents in America experience some form of bullying. Sadly, its practice doesn't end at school but extends now to social media and the workplace.

———————————————

Were you ever bullied at school?

Did you feel like your school administrators, teachers, and parents were aware of the bully problem at your school?

Do you remember any of the names of the bullies at your school?

Did anyone ever stand up to a bully at your school like they do in the movies?

Were you ever exposed to cyber-bullying?

Have you seen or experienced bullying as an adult?

What do you think are some ways that bullying can be exposed and dealt with?

What would you say to a child who was the victim of a bully at school?

BUYING A HOUSE

"The ache for home lives in all of us, the safe place where we can go as we are and not be questioned."

—Maya Angelou

"If I were asked to name the chief benefit of the house, I should say: the house shelters daydreaming, the house protects the dreamer, the house allows one to dream in peace."

—Gaston Bachelard

For most of us, buying a house is the biggest purchase we'll ever make. The average cost of a house in the USA is over $200,000, with some mortgages allowing us to pay back the loan over the course of 50 years.

Do you know what your parents paid for the house you grew up in?

How would you describe your dream home?

Do you ever watch TV shows where people are looking to buy or renovate a house?

Do you currently own a home or have plans to buy one?

What is your opinion of the tiny house movement?

Are you aware that in the early years of your mortgage almost all of your payment goes back to the bank as interest?

When would you think it would be wiser to rent a house versus buying one?

How much would you be willing to pay every month on your house payment?

CALLING

"The things you are passionate about are not random; they are your calling."

—Fabienne Fredrickson

"The way to find your calling is to look at the way you were created. Your gifts have not emerged by accident."

—Timothy Keller

The word *vocation* comes from Latin and means a "call or summons." When what you do is motivated by your life's purpose and passion, it becomes your calling.

Do you believe you have found your calling?

Did your parents have a purpose and passion that motivated them through life?

What would you say to someone who had a passion to do something but had absolutely no talent to do it?

Is there something you would do if you knew there was no way you could fail?

Is it possible that pursuing a calling is overrated and it would be better to pursue contentment and discipline?

Who is someone you believe has a clear and confirmed calling to follow?

Is it wise to make a distinction between your calling and your job?

What are the steps that you would encourage someone to take to discover and develop their calling?

CAMPING

"Of all the paths you take in life, make sure a few of them are dirt."

—John Muir

"Camping isn't really a vacation, but it sure makes for good memories."

—Julie Kieras

Camping brings out our primal values and strips away all the technology that disconnects us from simplicity. Sitting outside around a campfire forces us to reconnect with nature and each other.

Do you like camping?

Did you grow up camping with your family?

What would you say to someone who was considering camping for the first time?

What do you think about "glamping" (glamorous camping)?

When you think of camping, does it include a tent, a hammock, or a camping trailer?

What are some memories you have of sitting around a campfire?

Where are some of the places you have been camping?

Have you ever gone camping off the grid for an extended period of time?

What's one place you'd like to go camping?

What do you think camping can teach us?

CAREER

"I can't imagine anything more worthwhile than doing what I most love. And they pay me for it."
—Edgar Winter

"You must love your work, and not be always looking over the edge of it, wanting your play to begin."
—George Eliot

A career is a long journey in the same direction. It's a strategy to grow and progress in your chosen field with the goal of reaching its highest levels of achievement.

———————————————————

Do you believe you have chosen the right career?

What do you believe is the next important step forward in your career?

What is the highest position or accomplishment in your field?

How much do salaries pay at the highest level of your field?

What's the possibility that you will change careers sometime in the future?

Is it important in your field to go for more schooling or get an advanced degree?

Would you be willing to relocate if your career presented you with the opportunity?

Have you seen people put their career above everything else including their marriage and family?

Where would you like to be in your career in five years?

LOVE

"When the power of love overcomes the love of power, the world will know peace."

—Jimi Hendrix

"Love has nothing to do with what you are expecting to get—only with what you are expecting to give—which is everything."

—Katharine Hepburn

Valentine's Day—there's not much more that could be written about love. The world doesn't need more words, it needs love itself—love that dies to self, love that puts others first.

Do you believe you are loved?

Do you feel like you grew up in a loving family?

How do you know what love is?

Do you ever feel that you are unlovable?

Who are the people you love?

Is there someone who loves you so much that they would be willing to die for you?

Do you think some people confuse love with romance and sexual attraction?

What's one way you could be more loving this year?

Is there a family or couple whose love for each other you truly admire?

Is it possible to love someone too much?

CARS

"Cars are the sculptures of our everyday lives."
—Chris Bangle

"The cars we drive say a lot about us."
—Alexandra Paul

Cars are crazy things. For some, they are just a means to get from point A to point B. For others, a car is their identity, their wardrobe, their statement on life.

How important is a car?

Why did you purchase the car you currently drive?

Are you content with the car you drive, or are you hoping one day to buy your dream car?

If you could own any car in the world, which one would it be?

What car(s) did your parents have when you were growing up?

Do you believe your car makes a statement?

What's color is your favorite car color?

Do you buy new or used cars?

Would you keep a car until it falls apart or sell it while it still has some value?

Are you loyal to a particular brand of car?

How much work and research do you put into purchasing a car?

CARTOONS

"I really believe in the power of comics as an educational thing, even ones as silly as mine, because they're a gateway to the actual thing. They're like an easy entrance."

—Kate Beaton

"Comic books, to me, are fairy tales for grown-ups."

—Stan Lee

Cartoons and comic books serve as an entertaining bridge to advanced levels of storytelling. They can give you a taste for story that only grows with time.

Did you grow up watching cartoons on TV?

What were some of your favorite cartoons or comic books?

Did your parents keep you from watching or reading certain cartoons or comic books?

Are you a fan of superheroes?

Who is your favorite cartoon/comic book character?

What is your favorite feature-length animated film?

Is there a cartoonist or illustrator whose work you really admire?

Do you think all the violence you've observed watching cartoons has affected you?

Are there any cartoons that you don't think kids should be watching?

FEBRUARY 17

CELEBRATIONS

"Life should not only be lived; it should be celebrated."

—Osho

*"Celebration is a kind of food we all need in our lives, and
each individual brings a special recipe or offering, so that
together we will make a great feast."*

—Corita Kent

We ought to celebrate more. In ancient days they killed the fatted calf, prepared a massive feast, danced in the streets, and hosted a party that lasted a week.

Do you like to celebrate?

Was your family known for hosting big celebrations that included extended family?

What's the largest, most expensive celebration you have ever been to?

What are some important things in life we often fail to celebrate?

What's the most amazing wedding you've ever been to?

Is there something unusual or unique you've experienced at a celebration that you'd like to include in your own?

What's the best way to make a person feel celebrated?

Do you believe a funeral should be turned into a celebration of that person's life?

How do you like to be celebrated?

CHILDHOOD

"Contemplating childhood is like contemplating a beautiful region as one rides backwards; one really becomes aware of the beauty at that moment, that very instant, when it begins to vanish."

—Søren Kierkegaard

"When we are children we seldom think of the future. This innocence leaves us free to enjoy ourselves as few adults can. The day we fret about the future is the day we leave our childhood behind."

—Patrick Rothfuss

The best thing about childhood is the novelty of everything. The years of our childhood are filled with more wonder than all our other years combined.

Did you have a happy childhood?

What do you remember most about your childhood?

What do you miss most from your childhood?

Was there something that happened that was particularly difficult during your childhood?

Did you spend a lot of time pretending and playing make believe as a child?

Did you grow up believing in Santa, the Tooth Fairy, and the Easter Bunny?

What's one thing from your childhood that you wish every child could experience?

CHILDREN

"When my kids become wild and unruly, I use a nice, safe playpen. When they're finished, I climb out."
—Erma Bombeck

"Everyone should have kids. They are the greatest joy in the world. But they are also terrorists. You'll realize this as soon as they are born, and they start using sleep deprivation to break you."
—Ray Romano

Let's be honest, children are selfish and needy. Every time you turn around they want something to eat or need their diaper changed, but the love you feel for them is so amazing, all you can say is, "Bring it on!"

Do you like children?

How many children are in your family?

Would you like to have children someday?

What's something you think we all need to learn from children?

What do you believe is the proper way to discipline a child?

Were you forced to eat your vegetables as a child, and would you force your own children to do the same?

What's the most difficult thing about having children?

What's one thing your parents did when they raised you that wouldn't be part of your parenting practice?

How is it possible to stay young and hang on to the wonder that comes with being a child?

CHIVALRY

"The motto of chivalry is also the motto of wisdom; to serve all but love only one."

—Honoré de Balzac

"I heard that chivalry was dead, but I think it's just got a bad flu."

—Meg Ryan

Chivalry is a code of conduct that goes back to the 12th century and the Knights of the Round Table. A knight was expected to be a man of courage, honor, courtesy, and justice, always ready to help the weak.

Do you believe chivalry is dead?

Did a member of your family model for you the qualities of chivalry?

Do you celebrate the uniqueness of being female and the uniqueness or being male?

Do you see value in teaching chivalry in the classroom?

Why do you think chivalry has been given such a bad reputation?

Do you think being a chivalrous knight back then is any different than wanting to be a superhero now?

Who are some characters from books and movies that you believe are good models of chivalry?

What's one way to give chivalry a new start?

CITY LIFE / COUNTRY LIFE

"The city seen from the Queensboro Bridge is always the city seen for the first time, in its first wild promise of all the mystery and the beauty in the world."

—F. Scott Fitzgerald

"What I learned growing up on the farm was a way of life that was centered on hard work, and on faith and on thrift. Those values have stuck with me my whole life. "

—Rick Perry

There are benefits to living in the city and benefits to living in the country. You have to decide if the benefits outweigh the negatives wherever you chose to live.

Are you a city person or a country person?

Did you grow up in the city or the country?

What do you think are the biggest benefits of living in the city?

What do you think are the biggest benefits of living in the country?

What could persuade you to switch from one place to the other?

What's one thing you envy about the other location?

Do you think you live with stereotypes or bias toward people who live in a different context and culture?

Do you enjoy visiting the city if you live in the country, or the country if you live in the city?

POWER

"Most people can bear adversity; but if you wish to know what a man really is, give him power."

—Robert Green Ingersoll

"Power is always dangerous. Power attracts the worst and corrupts the best."

—Edward Abbey

Today is George Washington's birthday. He would have hardly thought of himself as the head of a world power, but today, to be the president of the USA arguably makes you the most powerful person in the world.

———————————————

Do you believe you have power?

Who or what do you believe has power over you?

Why do people lust for power?

Do you believe there is someone who has demonstrated how to wisely steward great power?

Is there someone in power right now that makes you nervous?

What do you believe to be the greatest abuse of power of all time?

Do you believe that the three branches of the U.S. government do a good job of balancing power?

What's one thing we can do in the world to give power to the powerless?

CLEANLINESS

"Excuse the mess, but we live here."

—Roseanne Barr

"Better keep yourself clean and bright; you are the window through which you must see the world."

—George Bernard Shaw

Whether it's right or wrong, you will be judged by your appearance, your hygiene, your haircut, and the cleanliness of your car.

Would you consider yourself as one who values cleanliness?

How did your parents handle issues of cleanliness and order in your home?

Do you have a weekly house cleaning schedule that you follow?

Who is the biggest neat freak you know?

Is there one particular area of your life that needs to be clean and in order?

Do you have favorite cleaning products and fragrances?

When's the last time you washed and vacuumed your car?

Would you consider hiring a cleaning service if you had the money?

Do you find yourself judging people by the condition of their house, lawn, or car?

CLOTHING

"It's not about the dress you wear but the life you lead in the dress."

—Diana Vreeland

"You can have anything you want in life if you dress for it."

—Edith Head

They say "don't judge a book by its cover," but it's hard not to judge people by what they wear. Some people just don't care what they wear; others care too much.

How important are clothes?

Were your parents fashion-conscious?

What's the first brand of clothing that caught your attention?

How old were you when you first started thinking about your clothes?

What's the most expensive piece of clothing you own?

Are you drawn to certain colors, fabrics, or styles?

How many pairs of shoes do you own?

Is there a fashion designer or brand of clothing that you prefer?

Who has influenced your style of dress and your fashion choices?

Would you ever consider wearing second-hand or thrift store clothing to save money?

COLLEGE

"Education is the most powerful weapon which you can use to change the world."

—Nelson Mandela

"The things taught in schools and colleges are not an education, but the means to an education."

—Ralph Waldo Emerson

Experts are predicting that college as we know it will soon be a thing of the past, but it's hard to imagine a life without the fun of campus life, college sports, and the cultural center a college or university represents.

Is going to college important to you?

Did both your parents go to college?

Did your family stress the importance of a college education?

Where did you go (or plan to go) to college?

What are your feelings about the rising cost of a college education and the debt that goes with it?

Did you ever think it would be wiser to buy a house than pay the same amount for a college degree?

What are some of the benefits of college that go beyond academics and the classroom?

What do you see as the pros and cons of going to a big Division I school rather than a smaller college?

COLOR

"Of all God's gifts to the sighted man, color is holiest, the most divine, the most solemn."

—John Ruskin

"Color! What a deep and mysterious language, the language of dreams."

—Paul Gauguin

It's hard to imagine a world without color. It's what makes a sunset a sunset. Color is the pride of every peacock and the glory of every rose.

What's your favorite color?

Does color play a big part in what you buy?

Can you mix and match colors well?

When did you learn about the color wheel and primary colors?

Do you remember mixing paint to make new colors?

What was the most colorful moment of your life?

Is there an animal whose color and markings you find captivating?

Is there a fine artist whose use of colors you find exquisite?

Do you believe that certain colors hold meaning and significance?

What's one space in your life that could benefit from the presence of more color?

COMFORT FOOD

"My number one elixir for anxiety? Comfort food."

—Katie Lee

"Food, like a loving touch or a glimpse of divine power, has that ability to comfort."

—Norman Kolpas

Comfort food is like a teddy bear for your tummy. It's warm and fuzzy and feels safe and satisfying. It takes you to your happy place and fills your stomach, too.

What's your favorite comfort food?

Did you grow up having a certain meal on a certain night?

Is there one dish or meal your mom or grandma used to make that makes you weak in the knees?

What's your favorite take-out restaurant?

Do you have different comfort foods for different moods and different activities?

Is it possible that pizza, ice cream, and chocolate chip cookies are not on your list of comfort foods?

What's the strangest comfort food of someone you know?

If you could invent a new comfort food, what would be the main ingredients?

How often do you find yourself turning to your favorite comfort food?

COMPARISON

"Comparison is the thief of joy."

—Theodore Roosevelt

"Comparison with myself brings improvement; comparison with others brings discontent."

—Betty Jamie Chung

People always say to stop comparing yourself with others, but isn't that what they do when you interview for a job or apply for a grant?

Do you have a habit of comparing yourself to others?

Did your parents compare you with your siblings, cousins, or friends?

Have you learned to compete with yourself and pursue your own personal goals?

Do you think that some comparison is good?

What do you think of the "everyone gets a trophy" movement?

What's one area of your life that would improve if you could just stop comparing yourself to someone else?

What's one sport, hobby, or activity you could take up to improve yourself and set your own goals?

What's one way you can stop comparing people and start seeing them as individuals with unique strengths?

COMPETITION

"I have been up against tough competition all my life. I wouldn't know how to get along without it."
— Walt Disney

"The ultimate victory in competition is derived from the inner satisfaction of knowing that you have done your best and that you have gotten the most out of what you had to give.
— Howard Cosell

Competition is the motivation that drives athletic drama and business endeavors. It is also the motivation behind steroids and fraud.

Are you competitive by nature?

Did your parents sign you up for team sports as a child?

When was the first time you wanted to win or feared that you might lose?

How have organized sports helped you develop as person?

Do you have a favorite professional or college athletic team?

Do you enjoy watching the Olympics or the World Cup soccer tournament?

If not sports, in what other areas do you find yourself competing to win?

Do you feel like you have learned to win and lose gracefully, or do you still gloat and pout?

COMPLAINING

"Be grateful for what you have and stop complaining—it bores everybody else, does you no good, and doesn't solve any problems."

—Zig Ziglar

"The tendency to whining and complaining may be taken as the surest sign symptom of little souls and inferior intellects."

—Lord Jeffrey

Complaining is an irritating practice. The squeaky wheel may succeed in getting the grease, but it has also succeeded in earning the reputation of being that nasty old wheel that squeaks.

Do you think you are a complainer?

Is it possible to complain in a positive way?

Is there someone in your life who never complains?

Have you ever filed a formal complaint against someone or some situation?

Do you find yourself complaining about things that can't be changed, like the weather?

Have you ever met someone who complains so much that it's difficult to be around them?

Do you know of a situation where complaining has brought about positive change?

What would you tell someone if they wanted to learn an effective way to complain?

COMPROMISE

"Let your love be stronger than your hate or anger. Learn the wisdom of compromise, for it is better to bend a little than to break."

—H.G. Wells

"All compromise is based on give and take, but there can be no give and take on fundamentals. Any compromise on mere fundamentals is a surrender. For it is all give and not take."

—Mahatma Gandhi

A good compromise forces us to determine what is essential. Healthy compromise forces both parties to sacrifice, but neither one of the two has to die.

Do you see compromise as a positive or negative thing?

What did your parents teach you about compromise and making compromises?

Have you ever observed a situation where a compromise has brought about devastating results?

Can you describe a time when your willingness to compromise brought about a positive result?

Are you currently living in a situation that represents an unhealthy compromise?

How do you learn the difference between a healthy and an unhealthy compromise?

Is there someone whose unwillingness to compromise has earned your respect?

What's one thing that you will never compromise?

COMPUTERS

"Computers have lots of memory but no imagination."

—Bill Gates

"Computers are incredibly fast, accurate, and stupid: humans are incredibly slow, inaccurate, and brilliant; together they are powerful beyond imagination."

—Leo Cherne

What does it mean to be intelligent? It's impressive for a computer to speak many languages and calculate massive facts and figures, but intelligence goes beyond ones and zeros. True intelligence understands when, what, why, and how to love.

Do you enjoy working with computers?

PC or Mac?

When was the first time you used a computer?

Do you think we are becoming too dependent on computers?

How many hours a day do you spend looking at a computer or smartphone screen?

What do you believe to be the greatest benefit that computers have provided the human experience?

What software do you use and how does it help you?

Have you or someone you know ever considered disconnecting completely and going "off the grid"?

How can we be wise about the role of computers?

CONFRONTATION

"I have several times made a poor choice by avoiding a necessary confrontation."

—John Cleese

"If we confront someone, we should have one goal in mind: restoration, not embarrassment."

—Chuck Swindoll

When it comes to confrontation, the first thing you need to confront is your heart. If you're just angry and want to set someone straight, you're in for a train wreck.

Are you someone who avoids confrontation?

When was the last time you felt the need to confront someone on an important issue?

Do you know someone who does confrontation well?

When was the last time someone confronted you about an issue, and how did you handle it?

Is there someone you know who avoids confrontation at all costs, even to the point of making things worse?

Do you believe healthy confrontation is a skill that can be learned?

Have you ever been a part of a group confrontation toward a leader, an organization, or a company?

How is it possible to confront someone in a positive way when all you feel toward them is anger?

Do you have a confrontation story that has a happy ending?

CONNOISSEURS

"In our hurried world too little value is attached to the part of the connoisseur and dilettante."

—Edith Wharton

"The connoisseur does not drink wine but tastes its secrets."

—Salvador Dalí

A connoisseur is one who knows nuance, appreciates sophistication, and discerns excellence. A great connoisseur is never condescending but takes joy in sharing the superlatives of enjoyment.

What is something you enjoy so much it makes you want to be a connoisseur?

Do you believe it is possible to be a connoisseur without being a snob?

Is there someone who has contagiously shared their knowledge, affection, and enjoyment for something?

A connoisseur is usually a title given to someone who appreciates wine, haute cuisine, or the arts, but do you think it could extend to the appreciation of other things?

How would you describe the difference between a connoisseur and a fanatic?

What class or workshop would you like to take to help you appreciate something more?

How do questions help you become the "connoisseur" of yourself or someone else?

CONTENTMENT

"Contentment is the only real wealth."

—Alfred Nobel

"True contentment depends not upon what we have; a tub was large enough for Diogenes, but a world was too little for Alexander."

—Charles Caleb Colton

True contentment is difficult to achieve. If we're being honest, we have to admit our lives are far from perfect, and to be content with our imperfection only feels like giving in to mediocrity.

How would you describe your current level of contentment?

What do you believe are some things in life that give us a false sense of contentment?

Have you ever found yourself thinking if you only had a certain thing you would be content?

Can you think of someone you know who seems to be truly content?

Do you believe that there is wisdom in maintaining a healthy level of discontent with the status quo?

Was there a time in your life when you struggled with being content?

Is there something or someone that brought you contentment for a time but then stopped?

How do you feel your level of contentment affects the important relationships in your life?

CONTROL

"You cannot always control what goes on outside, but you can always control what goes on inside."

—Wayne Dyer

"If everything seems under control, you're just not going fast enough."

—Mario Andretti

Control is motivated by many things, including our fears, our ideals, and our need for power. What we seek to control reveals the true condition of our heart.

On a scale of 1-10, how would you rate your need for control?

Is there one area of your life that you would consider to be out of control?

What is one thing in your life that is outside of your control but that you desperately want to control?

Have you ever been affected by someone else's control issues?

Are there false thoughts or lies about yourself that seem to control you in negative ways?

How have you developed over the years in the area of self-control?

Do you believe that the only reason why things or people have control over us is because we give them permission?

Is there a moment in your life where you lost all control?

COOKING

"I think careful cooking is love, don't you? The loveliest thing you can cook for someone who's close to you is about as nice a valentine as you can give."

—Julia Child

"Cooking is like painting or writing a song. Just as there are only so many notes or colors, there are only so many flavors —it's how you combine them that sets you apart."

—Wolfgang Puck

Cooking is a basic skill, like learning to swim or riding a bike. You need it to survive, but once you get past the basics, cooking transforms the flavor of your life.

How much does cooking factor into your life?

Did your mom or dad love to cook and prepare special meals for your family?

What's a favorite meal or recipe that you love to prepare?

Do you have a favorite chef, cookbook, or cooking show that influences your cooking?

Is there a benefit to cooking at home versus taking the night off and going to a good restaurant?

Do you have any aspirations to be more than just a cook and become a *chef de cuisine*?

How important is it for you to have the right pots, pans, bowls, and other tools for cooking?

Do you have plans to cook a special meal in the near future?

COURAGE

"Man cannot discover new oceans unless he has the courage to lose sight of the shore."

—Andre Gide

"Courage is being scared to death...and saddling up anyway."

—John Wayne

You don't have to face death to be courageous. For some people, the decision to get out of bed in the morning is an expression of courage that would humble us all.

What do you think it means to be courageous?

Is being courageous something you can know beforehand, or is it only truly known only when it is required?

Would you be willing to share the story of someone you believe is truly courageous?

Do you believe that there are people who have been called courageous when they were really just lucky, reckless, or naive?

What's your favorite story, novel, or film that demonstrates the virtue of courage?

Have you ever been a coward?

Is there an area of your life that could benefit from an extra shot of courage?

How can we learn to be courageous?

COURTESY

"A tree is known by its fruit; a man by his deeds. A good deed is never lost; he who sows courtesy reaps friendship, and he who plants kindness gathers love."

—Saint Basil

"Courtesy is the one coin you can never have too much of or be stingy with."

—John Wanamaker

To be courteous is to be kind and generous without prejudice. It requires nothing of the recipient, for courtesy should not be extended on the basis of status or merit but on the worth and dignity of being human.

How important is it to be courteous?

Would you say that you are a person who goes out of their way to show courtesy?

Can you share a story where you observed one person extending courtesy to another?

Are there companies that you feel have distinguished themselves based on the quality of their customer service?

Would you share a story where you were treated in a discourteous way?

Do you associate courtesy with good manners, royalty, and the upper class?

How can we grow in our ability to be courteous?

Is there someone who might deserve a bit more courtesy from you?

MARCH 11

COVETOUSNESS

"And he said to them, 'Take care, and be on your guard against all covetousness, for one's life does not consist in the abundance of his possessions.' "

—Luke 12:15 ESV

"We do not covet anything from any nation except their respect."

—Winston Churchill

Covetousness is one of the "thou shalt nots." In its worst form, it's not just wanting a big house; it's wanting your neighbor to move out of that big house so you can move in.

How would you describe your struggle with covetousness?

Did you grow up hearing your parents talk about things that they wish they could have?

What's one thing you find yourself coveting?

Do you have any friends or family members who seem to always be struggling with wanting what they don't have?

When you were young, was there a toy or game that someone had that you wanted too?

Have you ever wanted something not because you wanted it but because someone else had it?

What's one thing you've been wanting for a long time that you might consider letting go?

CREATIVITY

"Creativity is the power to connect the seemingly unconnected."

—William Plommer

"Passion is one great force that unleashes creativity because if you're passionate about something, then you're more willing to take risks."

—Yo-Yo Ma

Creativity is the stuff of God. It is the ability to bring to life that which only exists in the mind of the maker. It's the ability to change the focus of your work from what is to what could be.

Do you consider yourself a creative person?

How did your parents encourage or discourage creativity in your home?

Do you feel that creativity is often hindered by stereotyping it as the work of artists and musicians?

Who is the most creative person you know?

Are there places you go or things that you do that bring out your creativity?

Do you use a journal to jot down or make drawings of your creative ideas?

What do you think about the debate that creativity is a discipline versus an inspired, muse-activated state?

What's one thing you could be doing this week to express yourself in a creative way?

CRITICISM

"I much prefer the sharpest criticism of a single intelligent man to the thoughtless approval of the masses."

—Johannes Kepler

"You can't let praise or criticism get to you. It's a weakness to get caught up in either one."

—John Wooden

Don't avoid criticism; instead, look for the right kind. Find someone who is wise, who has expertise, and who loves you enough to tell you the truth. That's the critic you're looking for.

How willing are you to accept criticism?

Would you characterize your family as being over-critical of you?

How hard are you on yourself?

Is there someone in your life who has proven to be a trusted and welcomed critic?

Was there a class, a job, or a boss that proved to be destructive in their criticism toward you?

Why do you think it's so easy to start with negative criticism instead of positive and constructive criticism?

Do you have different people help critique your work?

How do you think we can learn to be more effective in using constructive criticism to help people improve?

CRYING

"Crying is cleansing. There's a reason for tears, happiness or sadness."
—Dionne Warwick

"To me, when you're crying, you're aligned with some sort of truth. Some inner truth. That's why you cry. You identify. It's just ultimate honesty."
—Noah Centineo

Crying is a beautiful response to the realities of being human. Tears are our body's attempt to release all those overwhelming hurts and feelings that our souls can't contain and words can't express.

When was the last time you cried?

How did your parents handle crying in your home?

Do you find crying easy or hard for you?

How do you respond to sad movies?

Who's the biggest crier that you know?

Do you know someone who keeps it inside and doesn't let themselves have a good cry?

When was a time you had tears of joy?

Do you feel like it might be a good thing to challenge children not to cry so easily?

What's one thing in your life that could use a good cry?

DANCING

"The one thing that can solve most of our problems is dancing."

—James Brown

"Football isn't a contact sport; it's a collision sport. Dancing is a contact sport."

—Duffy Daugherty

Give yourself permission to dance—force yourself if you must. Dancing turns your heart into a can of pop: The more you shake it, the more joy bubbles out.

Do you like to dance?

Who taught you to dance?

Were your parents dancers, and did they encourage you to dance as a child?

What's your favorite music to dance to?

Live band or DJ?

Have you ever taken formal dance lessons?

Are you self-conscious, or can you dance like nobody is watching?

Did you ever have your own private dance parties in your bedroom to work out your moves?

When was the last time you went dancing, and do you think it's time to go again?

DARK NIGHT OF THE SOUL

"In a real dark night of the soul, it is always three o'clock in the morning, day after day."
—F. Scott Fitzgerald

"I believe the 'dark night of the soul' is a common spiritual experience. I believe too that the answer is continued seeking and perseverance. It helps to know that others have endured a loss of faith."
—Julia Cameron

In movies, the "dark night of the soul" refers to that scene just after the hero has received the ultimate death blow. You're all alone, defeated, and everything inside you says, "Just give up."

Do scenes from films come to mind when you think of "the dark night of the soul"?

Have you ever gone through a time in your life that you would characterize as a "dark night of the soul"?

Did you ever observe your parents or someone in your family go through an especially dark time?

Do you think life is like the movies—no matter how bad it gets, if you don't give up, the good guy will eventually win?

These deep, dark, low moments in a film are what create the drama of a great story. Do you think your lowest moments make your story good?

How can thinking of your life as a story or a film help you rethink the hard moments in your life?

110

ETHNICITY

"Ethnicity should enrich us; it should make us a unique people in our diversity and not be used to divide us."

—Ellen Johnson Sirleaf

"Maintaining one's culture, values, and traditions is beyond price."

—Getano Lui

Happy St. Patrick's Day! They call America the "melting pot," but may it never turn into a ubiquitous stew that hides all the flavor of our heritage and the Old Country.

Are you proud of your ethnic heritage?

In what ways was you ethnic background expressed in your home growing up?

Has anyone in your family immigrated to this country or another country to begin a new life?

Do you live in an ethnic-based community where most of the people share the same ethnic heritage?

Have you had the opportunity to enjoy a traditional meal or custom with a friend from a different ethnic background?

What's your favorite ethnic food other than your own?

Do you feel like globalization and the media are helping or hurting the expression of ethnic diversity?

Have you any interest in visiting the countries of your ancestors and learning their languages?

DATING

"To find a prince, you gotta kiss some toads."

—Foxy Brown

"The sea hath fish for every man."

—William Camden

Dating is fun, but be careful with your heart, for dating has a fatal flaw. Every relationship on the way to marriage has the potential to break your heart.

Do/did you enjoy dating?

What did you do on your first date?

Did your school or community host dances, balls, or a big prom celebration?

How old do you think someone should be to start dating?

Have you ever been exposed to the concept of courting?

Have you ever had your heart broken or broken someone's heart?

How would you describe the perfect date?

What is your opinion about online dating, speed dating, or any other form of non-traditional matchmaking?

Do you know married couples who still have a fun and active dating life?

DEATH

"I would rather die a meaningful death than to live a meaningless life."

—Corazon Aquino

"Some people die at 25 and aren't buried until 75."

—Benjamin Franklin

We avoid talking about death as much as we can. Death is painful, irreversible, and hard to understand. It forces us to question our purpose on earth and to consider the mystery of a life beyond.

Do you spend much time thinking about death and dying?

Are your parents and grandparents still living?

How do you and your family celebrate the people in your family who have passed away?

Buried or cremated?

Have you ever considered what might be the best way to die?

Do you believe in heaven and hell?

Is there something special that you would like to have someone say, present, or perform at your funeral?

Have you written a last will and testament expressing your final wishes?

Do you feel that we should force ourselves to spend more time discussing difficult topics like death?

DEBT

"A man in debt is so far a slave."
—Ralph Waldo Emerson

"Rather go to bed without dinner than to rise in debt."
—Benjamin Franklin

The average American has over $6,000 in credit card debt. If you include all debt, including mortgages, that figure rises to over $150,000. Avoid debt at all costs.

What's your personal position on debt?

Were you aware of the weight of debt in your family, and did it affect things at home?

Would you be willing to share how much debt you currently have?

What do you think about credit cards, and how often do you use one?

Have you ever taken a course or workshop on managing your finances?

Do you believe the banking industry has a moral obligation to inform their customers about the massive amounts of interest they charge?

Are you currently working to pay off a loan for school, a car, or a house?

How did you learn about managing your finances, the reality of interest, and the perils of debt?

DENTISTS

"Every time I go to the dentist they say, 'You really need to fix that gap of yours.' I'm like, 'My gap is paying your dentist bills.'"

—Lara Stone

"We have a zeal for laughter in most situations, give or take a dentist."

—Joseph Heller

Look for a dentist that treats your mouth like garden, tenderly weeding and helping your teeth grow. Run from the ones that see your mouth as a construction site, eager to pull out the jackhammer.

How do you feel about going to the dentist?

Were your parents vigilant about brushing your teeth and getting regular check-ups?

What was your first memory of going to the dentist?

Do you have many cavities?

Do you floss?

What's your favorite toothpaste?

Have you ever had any major dental work done, like a root canal?

Did you have to wear braces to straighten your teeth?

Do you like the condition of your teeth, and are you proud of your smile?

GOD

"If God did not exist, it would be necessary to invent Him."

—Voltaire

"Young man, young man, your arm's too short to box with God."

—James Weldon Johnson

People have lots of opinions about the existence of God. But if God does exist, we would be wise to spend some time considering what He thinks of us.

Do you believe in God?

Did you grow up in a family that went to church and believed in God?

What do you think God thinks about you?

Do you pray?

Have you ever had an encounter with God or the supernatural?

What would it take for someone who doesn't believe in God to change their mind?

Do you believe our thoughts and opinions about God should be forced on others?

How do you answer the question "If there's a God, why is there so much suffering in the world"?

Does God produce guilt, or does God produce love and grace?

DEPRESSION

"Depression is the inability to construct a future."

—Rollo May

"Depression is rage spread thin."

—George Santayana

Depression is a deep, dark hole without a bottom. Getting out has a lot to do with how far down you are— One foot? It's not too hard to climb out. A mile down? It's hard to imagine you'll ever see the light again.

What are the circumstances or things that cause you to get depressed?

Would you consider yourself someone who struggles with depression?

What are some ways you've found to cope with depression?

Is there a difference between melancholy, the blues, and depression?

Have you ever pursued counseling or medical attention to treat depression?

Do you know anyone who struggles with depression?

Are you able to sense when your friends are struggling with depression?

Why do you think so many people struggle with depression?

DESSERT

"Absolutely eat dessert first. The thing that you want to do the most, do that."

—Joss Whedon

"Creme Brulee is the ultimate 'guy' dessert. Make it and he'll follow you anywhere."

—Ina Garten

Dessert is like a story with a happy ending. The tale begins at the table: You must travel through the soup course, fight the evil peas, and then, in the last chapter, you're finally reunited with your true love—cake!

Are you a dessert person?

Do you practice a "dessert first" philosophy?

What was typically for dessert when you were growing up?

For dessert, do you prefer chocolate, fruit, or chocolate-covered fruit?

What's your favorite dessert of all time?

Were you ever punished with NO dessert?

Do you have dessert with most meals or only on special occasions?

Is there a dessert you've been wanting to try?

When's the last time you had dessert?

Are you someone who is willing to share your dessert?

DIETS

"Any woman who diets all the time can't help but be grouchy. Nobody can be amusing or entertaining on a diet."

—Zsa Zsa Gabor

"As for those grapefruit and buttermilk diets, I'll take roast chicken and dumplings."

—Hattie McDaniel

We're all on a diet—we all eat. The challenge is to eat the right things, but every day someone claims that yesterday's right thing to eat is today's wrong thing.

———————————————

Are you on a diet?

Are you worried about your weight?

What are some things you eat that make you feel great or feel lousy?

Are you concerned about the ingredients of the processed foods you eat?

What's the craziest diet you've ever heard of?

Is there someone in your life who tries every new fad diet or trend?

What's one thing you want to change regarding what you eat?

Is there one staple in your diet that you can't live without?

How would you summarize your philosophy of dieting?

DISAPPOINTMENT

"We must accept finite disappointment but never lose infinite hope."

—Martin Luther King, Jr.

"Disappointment is a sticky one, because no one can steal contentment, joy, gratitude, or peace—we have to give it away."

—Kristin Armstrong

The secret to avoiding disappointment is to have no expectations, but a life without expectation is a life without love. Accepting the risk of disappointment is what love requires.

Are you easily disappointed?

When was the last time you were deeply disappointed?

Do you remember a time when your mom or dad disappointed you?

What do you do when you are deeply disappointed with someone or something?

Do you feel that you are a disappointment to someone?

Do you believe in the saying "The expectation is always greater than the realization"?

What do you do to keep yourself from being disappointed?

Do you think we expect far too much from people and products?

MARCH 27

DISCIPLINE

"Discipline is doing what you really don't want to do so you can do what you really want to do."

—Jeff Fisher

"Discipline is the refining fire by which talent becomes ability."

—Roy L. Smith

Discipline is a practice that is easy to understand but difficult to consistently put into practice. What we need is the discipline to be more disciplined.

———————————————

Do you consider yourself to be a disciplined person?

Is there one positive habit or behavior that you consistently put into practice?

Who is someone who modeled discipline for you as a child?

In what area(s) of your life would you like to have more discipline?

What would you say is the key to having discipline?

Do you beat yourself up if you don't follow through on the things?

Who is the most disciplined person you know?

Is there one person, philosophy, or practice that informs your discipline and helps you grow?

DISCOURAGEMENT

"Discouragement is contagious and is easily transmitted to others."

—Max Anders

"Discouragement is not the absence of adequacy but the absence of courage."

—Neal A. Maxwell

It's reasonable and logical to feel discouraged, especially when you've fallen a thousand times. That's why it's important to fill your life with a thousand encouraging voices that say, "Get up! You can do it!"

———————————————

How do you battle discouragement?

Who or what has been the greatest source of encouragement in your life?

When was the last time you felt discouraged and wanted to give up?

Can recall a time when someone said or did something that was very discouraging to you?

Can you think of a time when a friend was deeply discouraged and you were able to encourage them?

Do you believe the discouraged are looking for company so they can all be discouraged together?

What is the greatest source of discouragement in your life right now?

DIVORCE

"In every marriage more than one week old, there are grounds for divorce. The trick is to find, and continue to find, grounds for marriage."

—Robert Anderson

"My wife Mary and I have been married for forty-seven years and not once have we had an argument serious enough to consider divorce; murder, yes, but divorce, never."

—Jack Benny

Divorce is devastating. When couples solemnly utter the words "until death do us part," they don't realize that divorce metaphorically fulfills that promise and something once beautiful has now died.

Are your parents still together?

How has divorce had an impact on your life?

Why do you think so many marriages end in divorce?

What if divorce wasn't an option?

How are the children of a broken marriage affected by their parent's choice?

Do you believe in pre-marital counseling?

How would you describe the most successful marriages that you have observed?

What's your solution to avoid the heartache of divorce?

DOCTORS

"The best doctors in the world are Doctor Diet, Doctor Quiet, and Doctor Merryman."
—Jonathan Swift

"The great secret of doctors, ... still hidden from the public, is that most things get better themselves; most things, in fact, are better in the morning."
—Lewis Thomas

Most doctors demonstrate great care and concern for their patients, but the practice of medicine is drifting off course. Pursuing wellness appears to have taken a back seat to pursuing procedure and treatment.

———————————

When was the last time you visited the doctor?

Do you have a primary care physician and annual physical exams?

What's your first memory of going to see a doctor, and was it a positive experience?

Do you know anyone who is a doctor or currently in medical school?

If you were to practice medicine, what area of specialization interests you most?

What is your opinion of the movement away from traditional medicine to a more holistic and natural approach?

Are you currently experiencing any physical concerns that should be checked out by a doctor?

DREAMS

"Hold fast to dreams, for if dreams die, life is a broken-winged bird that cannot fly."

—Langston Hughes

"All our dreams can come true, if we have the courage to pursue them."

—Walt Disney

When the dreams of our sleep become the dreams for our future, we can use our waking hours to pursue them and our sleeping hours to keep them alive.

What's one dream you have for your life?

Do you believe that dreams can come true?

Were you encouraged to follow your dreams as a child?

Do you know of someone who is pursuing a dream that seems to be impossible?

Is there one dream you've given up on?

Are you able to break down the steps necessary to see a goal or dream come true?

Do you think it is cruel to encourage a child's dream to play professional sports when it's obvious they don't have the talent or ability?

What's one dream you need to keep alive?

PRACTICAL JOKES

"Maybe the universe is a giant practical joke and we don't know the punchline."

—John Lloyd

"It is requisite for the relaxation of the mind that we make use, from time to time, of playful deeds and jokes."

—Thomas Aquinas

It's April Fool's Day, and somewhere out there, someone is putting salt in a sugar bowl, toothpaste in a donut, and a whoopee cushion under a teacher's seat.

———————————

Do you have plans to pull a prank on someone today?

Is April Fool's Day something you grow out of, or do the jokes just keep getting bigger and better?

What's the best trick anyone has ever played on you?

Are you easygoing, or do practical jokes make you furious and eager to get revenge?

Did your family observe April Fool's Day by playing tricks on one another?

Were you ever part of a practical joke or prank that crossed the line?

Have you ever used a whoopee cushion, a hand buzzer, or itching powder on someone?

What's a practical joke that would have a positive effect and give everyone a good laugh?

DRESSING UP

"Dressing up is like therapy; I feel better in myself when I've made an effort."

—Paloma Faith

"I think every young girl at some point in her early life wonders what it's like to be a princess. They like the idea of dressing up and the fun of it."

—Julie Andrews

Some people love dressing up, and others see it as a cruel form of punishment. A ball gown can be your worst nightmare, or your dream come true.

Do you like dressing up and going out?

When you were growing up, did you have "dress-up" clothes that you only wore to special events?

What's the most you've ever spent on a dress, a suit, or a pair of shoes?

Do you have a desire to go to a ball, a royal wedding, or a coronation?

Do you believe the way we think and feel about ourselves changes when we dress up in our best clothes?

Is there a dress, suit, or pair of shoes you've been wanting to purchase?

Do you believe that society has moved away from fancy dress-up events?

What do you wear when you want to be you?

EDUCATION

"Education is the most powerful weapon which you can use to change the world."

—Nelson Mandela

"Education is the movement from darkness to light."

—Allan Bloom

The purpose of education is not to pursue a better job but to pursue a better life. Education reveals choices you didn't know exist and develops an ability to discern the difference between good, better, and best.

———————————————

Is education important to you?

How did your parents inform your thinking about school and education?

What is something you're attempting to learn right now?

Are you open to getting more schooling or pursuing advanced degrees?

What was the best education you've received outside of the classroom?

Do you believe that traditional forms of education will be replaced with online, technology-driven courses?

What do you believe are the qualities and characteristics of a good education?

How much money should you be willing to spend on getting a good education?

ENDURANCE

"Endurance is not just the ability to bear a hard thing but to turn it into glory."

—William Barclay

"Endurance is patience concentrated."

—Thomas Carlyle

The secret of endurance is to make the body slave to the mind. When the mind is master, the body keeps going, but when the body is master, a voice gets in your head and starts demanding, "Stop, this hurts!"

When was the last time you had to demonstrate endurance?

How would you distinguish between physical endurance and mental endurance?

Have you ever wanted to run a marathon, a triathlon, or the Iron Man?

What's the longest you've ever done something without stopping?

Do you think there ever comes a point where endurance is destructive?

Who is someone in your life who has demonstrated endurance?

Is there something you gave up on but wish you would've continued?

How do we develop and grow our endurance?

ENERGY

"Passion is energy. Feel the power that comes from focusing on what excites you."

—Oprah Winfrey

"Energy and persistence conquer all things."

—Benjamin Franklin

Energy is the rocket fuel of hope. There are thousands of people with money and dreams, but they don't have the energy to get off the couch.

Do you have lots of energy?

Who is the most energetic person you know?

Would you say the level of energy you have is affected more by what you eat or by your attitude and how you feel?

Have you ever used coffee, energy drinks, or pills to get your energy back?

Do you believe in taking naps?

Is there someone you know who has been able to keep up high levels of energy even in old age?

What's one thing you always find energy to do?

Do believe a lack of energy can actually produce positive results, like finding a more efficient way to complete a task?

What activity gives you more energy as opposed to taking energy?

ENTREPRENEURS

"The entrepreneur always searches for change, responds to it, and exploits it as an opportunity."

—Peter Drucker

"My son is now an 'entrepreneur.' That's what you're called when you don't have a job."

—Ted Turner

Entrepreneur is a title that sounds amazing, but when you realize it requires great risk, endless hours, and swimming against the tide, most gladly pull out their résumé and start looking for a job.

———————————————

How would you rate your entrepreneurial spirit on a scale of 1-10?

Is there someone in your family who was a successful entrepreneur?

If you could start up a company you knew wouldn't fail, what company would you create?

Do you have a favorite start-up company?

What are the most attractive aspects of being an entrepreneur?

Do you think that most people who call themselves entrepreneurs are just really deluded?

If you had to give advice to a young entrepreneur, what would you tell them?

Who's your favorite entrepreneur?

APRIL 07

EPIPHANIES

"Gratitude bestows reverence, allowing us to encounter everyday epiphanies, those transcendent moments of awe that change forever how we experience life and the world."

—John Milton

"The inspiration can come in such small ways that if you sit there just waiting for the big epiphany you'll sit there for the rest of your life."

—Irvine Welsh

An epiphany is that single moment when you suddenly understand and become consciously aware of something that holds great importance.

Have you ever had an epiphany?

Do you have a spiritual association with the word *epiphany*, like hearing a voice from heaven or being visited by an angel?

Do you know anyone who has had a radical spiritual epiphany?

Have you had any "aha moments," like realizing there are people who never went to college who make a ton of money?

Is there someone in your life who could use a good epiphany right now?

Have you ever asked for a sign?

What's your favorite epiphany story where someone makes a great discovery or changes from bad to good?

ESCAPISM

"A great book provides escapism for me. The artistry and the creativity in a story are better than any drugs."

—Wentworth Miller

"James Bond was escapism, but not to be imitated in real life."

—Roger Moore

Escapism can be the healthy habit of taking a break to read a book. It can also represent the scary decision to stop facing reality.

What are your favorite forms of escape?

Are there some difficult things in your life that you need to confront as opposed to avoid?

Do you know of a friend or family member who is unwilling to confront the realities of life?

What would you consider to be some unhealthy forms of escapism?

What was the longest period of time you avoided the inevitable?

If you could escape to any place on the planet where would you go?

Have you ever had to confront someone about their escapism?

What are you planning to do on your next big escape?

APRIL 09

ETHNIC FOOD

"An Englishman teaching an American about food is like the blind leading the one-eyed."
—A. J. Liebling

"There's nothing more romantic than Italian food."
—Elisha Cuthbert

Tacos, egg rolls, cannolis, and gyros are all in the ethnic food hall of fame. The really good news is that the world is filled with new and exciting candidates, and it's our job to find them.

What is your favorite ethnic food?

Did your parents or grandparents prepare traditional recipes from your ethnic background?

Why do you think Chinese food, Mexican food, and Italian food are so popular all over the world?

What is the most unique ethnic food you've ever tasted?

What's your opinion of ethnic fast food restaurants like Taco Bell and Panda Express?

Do you have any favorite international recipes that you prepare at home?

Have you ever gone to an ethnic-fusion restaurant where the menu attempted to combine flavors and ingredients from two different countries?

If you could go anywhere, where would you go to eat ethnic food?

BROTHERS & SISTERS

"Siblings: children of the same parents, each of whom is perfectly normal until they get together."

—Sam Levenson

"What brothers say to tease their sisters has nothing to do with what they really think of them."

—Esther M. Friesner

Siblings Day is the day we celebrate our brothers and sisters. They are the friends we didn't choose and the frustration we'll never lose.

Do you have brothers and/or sisters?

Where do you fall in the birth order of your family?

Do you think it's hard to be an only child?

Are you closer to one sibling than another?

Do you have a brother or sister you don't really talk to anymore?

What's your fondest memory of being with your siblings?

How many children do you believe would be the right amount of siblings?

What's one thing parents do that brings siblings together or pulls them apart?

What could you do this year to bring your family closer together?

APRIL 11

EXERCISE

"The only way you get that fat off is to eat less and exercise more."

—Jack LaLanne

"To enjoy the glow of good health, you must exercise."

—Gene Tunney

Exercise is known as the "E" vitamin. It's the most effective way to stay healthy, feel good, and have more energy. It's also the hardest.

Do you exercise?

What's your favorite way to exercise?

Have you ever joined a gym, enrolled in an exercise class, or practiced yoga?

What is the worst exercise gimmick of all time?

Do you own a treadmill, stationary bike, or other piece of exercise equipment?

Who is your favorite exercise guru?

What's the longest period of time you have consistently kept to an exercise routine?

Do you know someone who is obsessed with fitness, exercise, and working out?

What do you think about working with a personal trainer to help you get in shape?

When is the next time you plan to exercise?

EXPERTISE

"Never become so much of an expert that you stop gaining expertise. View life as a continuous learning experience."

—Denis Waitley

"People who have expertise just love to share it. That's human nature."

—David Baldacci

Expertise is what distinguishes one person from another, and for some careers it's essential. Plastic surgery requires it, but scooping ice cream not so much.

Do you possess a level of expertise at something?

Does calling yourself an expert require that you have credentials?

What's one area of expertise that holds your highest level of respect?

Do you know someone who is world-class in their area of expertise?

What's one thing that may require expertise but represents a complete waste of time and effort?

If you could be an expert in anything, what would it be?

Are there things that you love to do that you are content not to master?

Is there one area in your life that could benefit from the advice of an expert?

EXTENDED FAMILY

"A family's photograph album is generally about the extended family, and, often, that is all that remains of it."

—Susan Sontag

"The only rock I know that stays steady, the only institution I know that works is the family."

—Lee Iacocca

Everyone has extended family, but not everyone chooses to put all those people in the same room. Extended family requires extended grace.

Do you have a good relationship with your extended family?

Would you say you come from a close family?

How many of your family members have been in the same place at the same time?

Does your family have regular family reunions?

Who is the oldest living member of your extended family?

Do have a special connection with someone in your extended family?

What is the most memorable party, wedding, or gathering you've had with your extended family?

How has your extended family demonstrated love and support for one another?

What's one thing you could do to grow your relationship with extended family members?

EXTROVERTS

"Extroverts never understand introverts, and it was like that in school days. I read recently that all of us can be defined in adult life by the way others perceived us in high school."

—Neil Peart

"Social media is an advertisement for the superficial extroverted self."

—Hozier

One benefit of being an extrovert is the joy of having many friends, but it's foolish to think it's better to have 1,000 friends over the deep joy of only having a few.

Are you an introvert or an extrovert?

Have you been guilty of believing that being an extrovert is better?

Who is the most extroverted person you know?

How can extroverts be especially annoying?

Are there situations when you are glad there are extroverts around?

Do you think that someone can grow to be an extrovert or develop a more outgoing personality?

Do you feel like the world values extroverts more than introverts?

Is there someone you know who would benefit from the understanding of what it means to be an extrovert?

FAILURE

"But man is not made for defeat. A man can be destroyed but not defeated."
—Ernest Hemingway

"It's fine to celebrate success, but it is more important to heed the lessons of failure."
—Bill Gates

Most people don't fear failure; they fear the pain that comes with it. How amazing it would be to invent a big foam mattress for all the failures in life, then we wouldn't be so afraid to just get up and try again.

———————————————

Are you afraid of failure?

What do you consider to be the greatest failure in your life?

How do you convince yourself to get up and try again after an especially painful failure?

Do you believe that someone thinks of you as a failure?

Is there someone who helped you see failure as the pathway to improvement?

What's one skill that you developed because you were not afraid of failing?

Is there someone in your life who is struggling with failure and could use your encouragement?

What's one thing in your life that you would like to achieve but the fear failure keeps you from pursuing it?

FAITH

"To one who has faith, no explanation is necessary. To one without faith, no explanation is possible."

—Thomas Aquinas

"Faith is to believe what you do not see; the reward of this faith is to see what you believe."

—St. Augustine

Faith is believing in something even when there's no physical evidence to prove it. It's an invisible argument you believe in your heart, and from the beginning, it's been something people have been willing to die for.

———————————————

What is something or someone you have faith in?

Do you have faith in yourself?

Who were the ones who had faith in you even when you didn't?

Would you consider yourself to be religious?

Is there someone whose faith in God has impressed you?

Do you believe that most people are naive and put their faith in things they shouldn't?

Is there a book or movie that has inspired your faith?

Would you like to grow in your faith?

Is there something in your life that you have every reason to doubt but somehow in your heart you still believe?

FAMILY OF ORIGIN

"For me, what I try to heal is the major thing that I think all of us go through, where we come from. From our family of origin."
—Giancarlo Esposito

"I think that in any family—black, white, Chinese, Spanish, whatever—family is family. You know that there's dysfunction, and that there's this cousin who doesn't like this auntie. But, at the end of the day, like I say, love brings everybody together."
—Lauren London

Your "family of origin" are the relatives you grew up with, and these are the people who established the unwritten rules of your world. The trouble is when two people get married, these two worlds collide.

What's one unique thing you do, think, or believe because of your family of origin?

Have you rejected anything that was valued or practiced in your family as a child?

What's one thing you've observed in another family that you wish would've been a part of your family of origin?

How would you describe the process of making decisions in your family?

Was there a particular way of doing things in your family that you would like to keep alive?

Do you believe that most people are aware of how their families have influenced their perception of the world?

FAST FOOD

"Fast food is popular because it's convenient, it's cheap, and it tastes good. But the real cost of eating fast food never appears on the menu."
—Eric Schlosser

"The problem is when that fun stuff becomes the habit. And I think that's what's happened in our culture. Fast food has become the everyday meal."
—Michelle Obama

We love fast food because it's cheap, fast, and injected with flavor. We convince ourselves that it's saving us time and money, but fast food always makes our body pay in other ways.

How often do you eat fast food?

What's your fast food destination of choice?

Did your parents take you out for fast food?

Do you believe that fast food restaurants have done enough to improve their food and educate their customers?

Do you already know what you're going to order before you even go to a fast food restaurant?

Have you ever worked at a fast food restaurant?

Do you usually use the drive-through or eat inside?

What do you usually spend for a meal at a fast food restaurant?

Are you okay with the amount of fast food you eat?

FATAL FLAW

"Better a diamond with a flaw than a pebble without."

—Confucius

"I like the fact that in ancient Chinese art the great painters always included a deliberate flaw in their work: human creation is never perfect."

—Madeleine L'Engle

It started with Achilles' heel and Superman's kryptonite. All heroes have a fatal flaw, and so do we. It's that one weakness we wish would go away, and we pray that no one ever finds out what it is.

What's your fatal flaw?

When you were a kid, did your family and friends know exactly how to bring you down?

How do you hide your greatest flaws?

Do you believe your greatest weakness can also represent your greatest opportunity for growth?

Why is it important in a story for the superhero to have a fatal flaw?

Have you been able to accept the major flaws of those closest to you?

What has helped you the most in your battle against your greatest weaknesses?

Do you believe that social media produces an obsession with hiding our flaws?

FAVORITE PHOTOGRAPH

"A true photograph need not be explained; nor can it be contained in words."

—Ansel Adams

"My mother's favorite photograph was one of herself at twenty-four years old, unbearably beautiful, utterly glamorous, in a black-straw cartwheel hat, dark-red lipstick, and a smart black suit, her notepad on a cocktail table. I know nothing about that woman."

—Amy Bloom

A photograph captures a moment, and some moments are better than others. We all have that one photograph that captures our best moment of all.

Do you have a favorite photograph?

How many photographs do you have of yourself as a baby?

Would you describe yourself as photogenic?

Is there a photograph of someone or some place that is especially meaningful to you?

Are there some photographs that you would like to destroy?

Do prefer digital images or printed photographs?

Who is the keeper of all the family photographs and videos?

Are you someone who is always taking pictures at parties and family gatherings?

Do you have a greater understanding of who you are based on the photographs of a younger you?

FAVORITE SCENE

"When I look at my favorite films, the Frank Capra—even Scorsese, even Goodfellas, what makes that movie so remarkable is there's enchantment in their world."

—David O. Russell

"One of my favorite things is to first read the novel and then see the movie. I enjoy picturing the characters and then later, seeing them on the screen, comparing how they're different."

—Camille Perri

There are moments in a movie that resonate deeply. Somehow the screenwriter imagines a unique human moment we thought no one else ever knew.

What's your favorite scene from a movie?

Is there a scene from a movie that reminds you of something that happened to you?

Do you believe that scenes from a movie can give us a distorted view of reality?

What's the funniest movie scene of all time?

Is there a romantic moment in a movie that makes you cry?

Do you find yourself using lines from a movie with your friends or family?

What do you think is the most famous movie line of all time?

Is there one film you watch over and over just to see one scene?

ENVIRONMENTALISM

"A true conservationist is a man who knows that the world is not given by his fathers, but borrowed from his children."

—John James Audubon

"Water and air, the two essential fluids on which all life depends, have become global garbage cans."

—Jacques Yves Cousteau

Seeing the earth from space for the first time put a whole new perspective on environmentalism. We realized from those photographs that our world is finite, small, and it needs to be protected.

Are you passionate about protecting our environment?

Have you had the opportunity to visit some of the world's greatest natural wonders?

Is there one issue regarding our environment that concerns you most?

What are your thoughts about global warming?

Do you believe that the electric car will replace fossil fuel vehicles within your lifetime?

What books, films, or television shows have inspired you regarding the protection of our planet?

Have you ever taken a class on protecting the environment?

Is there one organization you believe is doing an excellent job in protecting the environment?

FAVORITE TOY

"To this day, I have the most fond memories of some of my old toys."

—Michael Keaton

"As men get older, the toys get more expensive."

—Marvin Davis

Milne gave us Pooh Bear, and Pixar gave us Woody. Every child seems to form a special bond with a stuffed animal or rocket ship. Somehow, a day comes when that toy mysteriously disappears.

Did you have a favorite toy as a child?

Do you remember a special toy you received for your birthday or Christmas?

Did the toys you played with center around imaginary creatures, building things, or tea parties?

Was there a toy you asked for but never received?

What happened to all your childhood toys?

Was there a set of toys that you collected?

What do you think is a reasonable amount of money to spend on a toy for a little child?

Were you ever jealous of someone else's toy collection?

How do you think toys have changed over the years?

Do still like toys, just more expensive ones?

FEAR

"The only thing we have to fear is fear itself."

—Franklin D. Roosevelt

"The oldest and strongest emotion of mankind is fear, and the oldest and strongest kind of fear is fear of the unknown."

—H.P. Lovecraft

Fear is that terrible feeling that comes when we think something good is going to end. But consider the opposite. We should fear the contentment that keeps us from pursuing something better.

Would you consider yourself a fearful person?

What are your greatest fears?

What do you do to combat fear?

Have you ever thought you were going to die?

Do you like to be scared at haunted houses or by watching horror films?

What is the most irrational fear you've ever experienced?

Have you ever had to comfort someone who was afraid that something terrible was going to happen?

Is fear ever a good thing?

Has the fear of something bad happening caused you to take precautionary measures?

FIRST APARTMENT

"Everyone says buying your first apartment makes you feel like an adult. What no one mentions is that selling it turns you right back into a child."

—Anderson Cooper

"That first apartment was a big step. It has a lot to do with being independent."

—Irene Cara

You never feel more grown up than when you sign the lease on your first apartment. It's a rite of passage that demonstrates your sense of style and the limits of your bank account.

Describe your first apartment?

How much did you pay for rent?

Did you have roommates when you moved into your first apartment?

How long did you live in your first apartment, and what caused you to move out?

How did you furnish your first apartment—was it your parents' old furniture, thrift store, or IKEA?

What were the requirements for your first apartment—for cost, for location, for accommodations?

What's one thing that surprised you about the realities of being on your own?

Do you still have furniture, pictures, or appliances from your first apartment?

FIRST DAY OF SCHOOL

"I always loved the first day of school better than the last day of school. Firsts are best because they are beginnings."

—Jenny Han

"The first day of school—the day when the countdown to the last day of school begins."

—Unknown

The first day of school is a day filled with the word *new*—new clothes, new pencils, new teacher, and new friends. Best of all it's a brand new school year and the hope of better grades.

Do you remember your first day of school?

What was your kindergarten teacher like?

Was your first year of school a positive experience?

How many different schools did you attend between kindergarten and high school?

Is there something nostalgic about the beginning of a new school year?

Did your parents buy you new clothes at the beginning of each school year?

Was there a transition to a new grade that you were excited about, or one you dreaded?

Have you ever thought about going back to your old school?

FIRST JOB

"A new job is not a new beginning. It is a path to create a new ending."

—Unknown

"I learned to take the first job that you have in the business that you want to get into. It doesn't matter what that job is, you get your foot in the door."

—Wes Craven

First jobs aren't usually very glamorous, but they do represent first paychecks. It's the first time you realize someone has placed a value on an hour of your life.

What was your first job?

How much was your first hourly wage or annual salary?

Were you able to get a job in your chosen field of study?

Was there something particularly humbling about your first job?

Was there someone at your first job that looked out for you?

How long did you stay at your first job?

Who was your first boss and how did they treat you?

How many vacation days did you get your first year, and where did you go?

What advice would you give someone starting their first job?

FIRST MEMORIES

"I think everyone must have a first memory of some house, some room, a vivid picture that will remain deep down in one forever."

—Sister Parish

"I don't think I remember my first memory."

—Ellen DeGeneres

First memories are usually fuzzy, faint, and lacking detail. What most of us do remember with clarity is how we felt about the situation.

What is your earliest childhood memory?

Would you characterize your earliest memories as happy or sad?

Is there a building, room, or landmark that is part of those memories?

Is there a grandparent or great-grandparent that you remember who is no longer living?

Do you have any memories that might merely be the product of old photographs or home videos?

Do you ever get together with your family to talk about your early years?

What is your earliest memory of something you wore?

How vivid and detailed are your earliest memories?

FLAVOR

"If you combine good flavors, food turns into an orchestra."

—Joey Fatone

"Champagne has the taste of an apple peeled with a steel knife."

—Aldous Huxley

Flavor is a word usually used to describe how something tastes, but its usage has grown to describe the unique qualities of anything that can be enjoyed.

How would you describe your flavor preferences?

When was one of the first times in your life you realized that the flavor of something could make you happy?

What's the most disgusting thing you've ever tasted?

Is there a place in the world you particularly enjoy because of its local "flavor"?

Is there something you didn't like at first but developed an appreciation for its flavor?

Do you like to add flavors to coffee and other things to enhance their taste?

What flavor would characterize as being one of the most unique?

Is there a chef or restaurant that does unbelievable things with flavor?

If you could put one flavor in a bottle, which would it be?

FOOD

"There is no sincerer love than the love of food."

—George Bernard Shaw

"Spaghetti can be eaten most successfully if you inhale it like a vacuum cleaner."

—Sophia Loren

The classic question is "Do you eat to live, or do you live to eat?" I'm sure there's middle ground in there somewhere, but some delicacies are guilty of giving us a whole new reason to live.

———————————————

How important is food to you?

What's the longest time you have gone without eating?

Do you believe that some people have an addiction to food?

How much do you spend on food weekly?

How important to you is the quality or brand of the food you buy?

Where do you buy your groceries and why?

Paper or plastic?

How hard would it be to "go off the grid" and grow your own food?

What's one food you can't live without?

PRAYER

"Prayer is aligning ourselves with the purposes of God."

—E. Stanley Jones

"I had a mother who prayed for me, and prayer changes everything."

—Dennis Edwards

Prayer is talking to God. It's more than asking for the things we want. It's giving thanks, considering other's needs, and most importantly, listening.

What do you think about prayer?

Why do you think the United States of America has a National Day of Prayer?

As a child, did your bedtime routine include saying your prayers?

Have you ever experienced a time where you believe your prayers were answered?

Is there someone you know who seems to be deeply connected to God?

Is there someone who prays for you on a regular basis?

How do you think God feels when the only time people talk to Him is when they want something?

How can the practice of prayer become a more significant part of your life?

FORGIVENESS

"To forgive is to set a prisoner free and discover that the prisoner was you."

—Lewis B. Smedes

"To err is human; to forgive, divine."

—Alexander Pope

It's difficult to forgive, especially when someone hurts you intentionally. But forgiveness is more for you than for them; it's the first step to getting your life back.

When was the last time you had to forgive someone?

Is there an incident you can recall from your childhood where someone was cruel to you?

Were you forced to say you were sorry to your brothers, sisters, or friends?

Are you struggling to forgive yourself for something you've done?

Is there someone out there who owes you an apology, and do you think it will ever come?

Have you ever tried to make someone suffer by not extending your forgiveness right away?

What is the power of forgiveness?

Is there a relationship in your life that could be restored if the two of you could only forgive one another?

MAY 03

FRUSTRATION

"Frustration is fuel that can lead to the development of an innovative and useful idea."

—Marley Dias

"Expectation is the mother of all frustration."

—Antonio Banderas

Frustration is the dissonance that comes from having every indication that what we want is possible but for some annoying reason it's not happening.

How do you handle frustration?

How did your parents handle the frustrations of life?

Would you say that you are easily frustrated?

What's the most frustrating reality in your life right now that you can't change?

Is there a particular person who seems to be especially frustrating to you?

Have you ever caused someone great frustration?

Is there a particular situation that you always find frustrating, like being stuck in traffic or waiting in line?

What is one of life's most frustrating realities that you think should have been solved by now?

How can you grow and develop in your ability to cope with frustration?

FUN

"When you have confidence, you can have a lot of fun. And when you have fun, you can do amazing things."

—Joe Namath

"Even though you're grown up, you should never stop having fun."

—Nina Dobrey

Fun is one of the secrets to staying young. If it's still hard to wait until tomorrow because of all the fun you're going to have, you've got a great reason to keep living.

What do you do for fun?

What are some fun moments you recall from your childhood?

Who is someone in your life you admire because they are always making things fun?

How has your concept of fun changed over the years?

Is there one area of your life that seems to be completely devoid of fun?

Do you think work can be fun?

What's one thing that was fun when you were younger but now is no longer fun, and vice versa?

What's one thing you could do today that would be incredibly fun?

FUNERALS

"You know you're getting old when you go to more funerals than you do weddings."

—Jimmy Dean

"Always go to other people's funerals; otherwise they won't come to yours."

—Yogi Berra

Funerals don't do much for the person who died but often bring catharsis for those who live on. Funerals represent an opportunity to celebrate the life of someone we love and bring closure to their struggle.

When was the last time you went to a funeral?

What did you think the first time you ever went to a funeral?

Have you ever been to a funeral that felt more like a celebration party than a sad ceremony?

Do you know if you would like to be buried, cremated, scattered at sea, or blasted to space?

Is there something you would like to have someone say, sing, or do at your funeral?

Have you ever been in a class where the teacher asked you to write your own eulogy? What would you write?

How important to you is it to have your affairs in order, with a will in place and instructions for your funeral?

Are subjects like death and funerals topics you find difficult or uncomfortable to talk about?

GAMBLING

"Gambling: The sure way of getting nothing for something."

—Wilson Mizner

"Gambling has brought our family together. We had to move to a smaller house."

—Tommy Cooper

When you gamble and win, your body releases a chemical called dopamine that produces pleasure and elation. Gambling is not a drug, but it's the place you take yourself to get some.

Do you like to gamble?

Have you ever gone to a casino or taken a trip to Las Vegas?

What's the most you've ever won or lost gambling?

Did you grow up in a family that liked to play cards and other games of chance?

Have you ever made a bet with someone?

Is there someone you know who struggles with a gambling addiction?

Is there someone you know who is really good at gambling because they can count cards or figure out the odds?

Do you think gambling could be a good thing, that it demonstrates someone's willingness to take risks in life?

GENETICS

"Your genetics load the gun. Your lifestyle pulls the trigger."
—Mehmet Oz

"I'm one of those people you hate because of genetics. It's the truth."
—Brad Pitt

Life isn't fair, and our genes let us know it. Just remember, even though you're only 5' 2", it doesn't mean you can't play professional basketball.

How have your genetics given you an advantage in life?

In what ways has the physical body you were born with represent a disadvantage or struggle?

What's one thing about your body that you would like to change?

Do you think having all the physical qualities of a supermodel or NFL quarterback can be a disadvantage?

Is there someone you knew in high school who appeared to have it all because of how they looked?

Do you believe genetic testing should be used as a predictor for success, health, and career opportunity?

Would you be open to altering the DNA of a baby to avoid future disease and improve physical appearance?

In what way has a physical weakness or defect proven to be a catalyst for growth and perseverance in your life?

MOTHERS

"All that I am, or hope to be, I owe to my angel mother."

—Abraham Lincoln

"Some are kissing mothers and some are scolding mothers, but it is love just the same, and most mothers kiss and scold together."

—Pearl S. Buck

Mother's Day is celebrated the second Sunday of May, and it's spelled Mother's Day, not Mothers Day, the thought being that it should be less about mothers in general and more a day for celebrating your mom.

Do you make a big deal about Mother's Day?

What did your family usually do to celebrate Mother's Day?

How would you characterize your relationship with your mother?

Do you believe Mother's Day is just another greeting card holiday designed to shame us into spending money on cards and candy?

Have you ever considered how hard Mother's Day can be for those who have lost their mother or wish they could be one?

What do you think are some meaningful ways to celebrate our mothers?

How would you describe the impact a mother has on her children, and how is it different from that of a father?

GIFT GIVING

"One of the greatest gifts in life is giving time and giving love. It helps me to stay grateful and happy."
—Claire Holt

"In suggesting gifts: Money is appropriate, and one size fits all."
—William Randolph Hearst

Meaningful gift giving is an art form, and the gift card has done it great harm. A thoughtful gift is less concerned with what someone wants and more interested in making a connection with their soul.

What is the first gift you remember receiving as a child?

How did your parents practice gift giving at birthdays and holidays?

What was the most memorable gift you have ever received?

Is there a gift you have given to someone that you believe was especially meaningful?

What are the kind of gifts that always catch your attention and make you smile?

What is the strangest gift you've ever received or given?

How do you feel about the commercialization of holidays and extravagant gift giving?

Do you believe that it is truly more blessed to give than to receive?

GOALS

"One way to keep momentum going is to have constantly greater goals."

—Michael Korda

"Setting goals is the first step in turning the invisible into the visible."

—Tony Robbins

Goals are good, but choose them wisely. There's nothing worse than pursuing a goal your whole life only to find its achievement brings no satisfaction.

Do you have goals?

What is one significant goal you have been able to achieve in the last three years?

What do you believe is your most significant long-term goal?

Are you currently pursuing a goal that you believe is poorly motivated and should be abandoned?

Do you believe that setting a goal, writing it down, or saying it out loud affects the probability of its achievement?

What is the difference between a good goal and a bad goal?

Is there a date or deadline in your future that has a personal goal attached to it?

What's one goal you can establish today that will bring about the most positive benefit in one year's time?

GOING FOR A WALK

"If you are in a bad mood, go for a walk. If you are still in a bad mood, go for another walk."

—Hippocrates

"Everything is within walking distance if you have the time."

—Steven Wright

Going for a walk produces creative ideas, helps you problem solve, and reduces stress. Evidence also exists that a walk might even be good for your health.

Do you enjoy going for walks?

When you go for a walk, do you like to walk alone or do you appreciate the company of a friend?

Is there someone influential in your life who has been an advocate for the practice of taking a walk?

When you walk do you like to walk in silence, carry on a conversation, or listen to music or a podcast?

Can you recall any particularly memorable walks where you came to an important conclusion or had a revelation?

Is there a beautiful place somewhere in the world where you would like to take a walk?

Is there a time of day that you believe is more suitable for taking a walk?

What's keeping you from taking a walk today?

GOING OFF THE GRID

"And into the forest I go, to lose my mind and find my soul."

—Unknown

"Going off the grid is always good for me. It's the way that I've started books and finished books and gotten myself out of deadline dooms and things."

—Neil Gaiman

As technology becomes increasingly pervasive, we marvel at our willingness to give up so much control for small comforts and efficiency. People are rejecting this way of life more and more each day.

Have you ever considered living off the grid?

What is "the grid"?

What is the number one reason people chose to "disconnect" and live off the land?

Does it concern you that so much of life is controlled by the government and large corporations?

Do you think living off the grid is all or nothing, or are there less drastic ways to achieve the desired results?

What would be the one thing you would miss most living off the grid?

What would be the greatest benefit of living off the grid?

GOOD MANNERS

"The hardest job kids face today is learning good manners without seeing any."

—Fred Astaire

"Good manners will open doors that the best education cannot."

—Clarence Thomas

Good manners are a sure sign that someone appreciated you enough to teach you how to appreciate yourself and appreciate others.

How important is it for you to have good manners?

Did your parents require you to demonstrate good manners and address adults with respect?

Have you ever taken a manners class or a course in proper etiquette?

Do you have any pet peeves when it comes to behavior that demonstrates poor taste and the opposite of good manners?

Do you think today's younger generation lacks good manners?

What's the one thing someone can do to impress you with their good manners?

Do you like going to places where there is a high expectation for following protocols of etiquette and good manners?

What's one area that you would like to work on this year as it relates to having good manners?

A GOOD MEMORY

"Tell the truth because then you don't have to have a good memory."

—Jesse Ventura

"You never realize what a good memory you have until you try to forget something."

—Franklin P. Jones

They say that having a good memory is less important ever since the Internet, but I don't think anyone is interested in a doctor who responds, "Give me a second, I need to google that."

Do you believe you have a good memory?

Would you characterize your education as the memorization of important facts, dates, figures, and names?

With instant access to information on the Internet, do you believe intelligence has to be redefined?

Is there a poem, verse, or speech that you memorized as a child that you still remember?

What is something you think is still important to memorize by heart?

Have you ever tried to improve your memory?

Do you use tricks or mnemonic devices to help you recall important information?

What's one thing you've memorized that you hope you'll never forget?

GOOD TASTE

"Good taste is the modesty of the mind; that is why it cannot be either imitated or acquired."

—Delphine de Girardin

"Good taste is the worst vice ever invented."

—Edith Sitwell

Having good taste is a blessing and a curse. It's a gift to discern and enjoy the finer things of life. It also ruins any chance of being content with lesser things.

Would you say that you have good taste?

Who was the first person to demonstrate good taste and an appreciation for the finer things?

Do you think it is possible to have good taste without being pompous and arrogant?

What's one thing you enjoy that represents a level of good taste and sophistication?

Do you think good taste requires a lot of money?

What would your checkbook or credit card statement reveal about your taste?

Do you ever wish that you could be content with things that were lower quality?

If you could take a class to grow in your appreciation for something, what would it be?

Are you known for your good taste in something?

MAY 16

GOSSIP

"Gossip is the Devil's radio."

—George Harrison

"Fire and swords are slow engines of destruction, compared to the tongue of gossip."

—Richard Steele

Gossip is a sure sign of insecurity. It seeks to publicize the struggles and misfortune of others and attempts to cast dispersion and judgment on their good fortune and successes as well.

Are you prone to gossip?

Do you have the ability to discern between genuine concern and gossip?

Have you ever been the victim of gossip or terrible rumors?

What do you think makes gossip so tempting and widespread?

How do you shut down a conversation when someone comes to you with an especially juicy piece of gossip?

Have you ever heard a rumor but instead of spreading it decided to ask the victim if the rumor was true?

Are you part of a community or circle of friends that refuses to gossip?

What would you like a true friend to do if they heard rumors or gossip about you?

GRACE

"Grace means that all of your mistakes now serve a purpose instead of serving shame."

—Brené Brown

"God's mercy and grace give me hope—for myself, and for our world."

—Billy Graham

Grace is to extend love, mercy, and forgiveness even though a just and logical response would be to accuse, pass judgment, and condemn.

When was the last time you experienced grace?

Do you consider yourself to be a person who easily extends grace?

Is there a downside to grace?

Are you familiar with the song "Amazing Grace," and if so, what does it mean to you?

How is the word *grace* different when used to describe movement and style, as in "a graceful dancer"?

Is there a situation in your life that might benefit from grace being offered to you or extended by you?

Do you have a favorite novel, play, or film that illustrates an amazing act of grace?

Do you believe it is possible for someone to grow in their ability to extend or accept grace?

GRANDFATHERS

"Every generation revolts against its fathers and makes friends with its grandfathers."

—Lewis Mumford

"A baby has a way of making a man out of his father and a boy out of his grandfather."

—Angie Papdakis

Grandfathers have a profound way of sharing two of life's most important lessons. The first is that life is short, and the second is that we are not merely individuals but the product of generations.

Are your grandfathers still alive and in good health?

How would you describe your relationship with your grandfathers?

How do you like to spend time with your grandfathers?

Do either of your grandfathers have a quirky habit or strange way of doing things?

What are some characteristics of your grandfather that you see in your parents or yourself?

Is there one thing your grandfather did that you would also like to do?

What do you think are the qualities of a good grandfather?

Is there one thing you need to do or wish you would have done with your grandfather before he passes?

GREATEST OF ALL TIME

"Fifty years from now I'll be just three inches of type in a record book."
—Brooks Robinson (best third baseman of all time)

"I am the greatest. I said that even before I was."

—Muhammad Ali

The people and things we regard to be the greatest of all time are always up for debate. There's an immediate connection when we agree and a passionate argument for us to enjoy when we don't.

———————————————

Do you have some people you hold up as the best of all time at what they did?

Do you have an ongoing debate over the superiority of one thing or one person over another?

What do you think are some of the most popular "greatest of all time" debates?

Who was the greatest singer or musician of all time?

What athlete or athletic team do you believe was the greatest of all time?

Do you believe it's a worthwhile goal to be the greatest of all time at something?

If you could be the greatest of all time at something, what would it be?

Who was the greatest person of all time?

GROWING OLD

"Beautiful young people are accidents of nature, but beautiful old people are works of art."

—Eleanor Roosevelt

"Being young is beautiful, but being old is comfortable."

—Will Rogers

Growing old gracefully is an elusive thing. It hinges on your health and the strength of your body. It also hinges on your purpose and motive to live.

Do people in your family age gracefully?

What do you think is the most difficult thing about growing old?

Who is the oldest living person in your family?

How long would you like to live?

Do you ever think about retirement and what you would like to be doing in your old age?

Who is someone you admire for how they have taken care of themselves and adapted to growing old?

Which ability will you grieve the most when it's gone?

Do you believe that growing old gracefully is a choice, and if so, what choices affect how you age?

GULLIBILITY

"Youth is easily deceived because it is quick to hope."

—Aristotle

"Be open-minded, but not so open-minded that your brains fall out."

—Groucho Marx

Why would anyone lie or seek to take advantage? What would the world be like if everyone just told the truth? Taking advantage of someone's gullibility seems like a cheap way to get ahead.

Do you consider yourself to be gullible?

Have you ever been guilty of taking advantage of a someone who was easily deceived?

Do you think that taking advantage of gullible people when they are young is society's way of teaching them to beware?

Are there companies that you believe have unethically taken advantage of gullible people, like high-interest credit cards?

Do you remember a time in your life when you were fooled and you said to yourself, "Never again"?

Who is the most gullible person you know?

Can you think of any widely accepted beliefs and practices that demonstrate gullibility on a global scale?

Have you ever felt a conviction to inform, teach, or protest a message that preys on people's gullibility?

GUNS

"The world is filled with violence. Because criminals carry guns, we decent law-abiding citizens should also have guns. Otherwise they will win and the decent people will loose."

—James Earl Jones

"Guns are evil! And very little good comes from the availability of a bullet designed to kill human beings!"

—Mackenzie Astin

Nothing divides a room faster than the topic of guns and gun control. Nothing makes a person want to hold on to their gun tighter than a person who wants to forcefully take it away.

How do you feel about guns and gun control?

Did you grow up in a family that had guns?

Have you ever been hunting, to a firing range, or skeet shooting?

What was the motivation and purpose behind the 2nd Amendment? Do you believe it's still relevant today?

What do you think about the argument that gun control only takes guns away from the good guys?

Do you own a gun?

What do you believe is the best way for someone to defend themselves if someone breaks into their home?

Do you have a solution for all the shootings and violence in the world today?

GYM CLASS

"Gym class was, of course, where the strongest, best-looking kids were made captains and chose us spazzes last."

—Ayelet Waldman

"I can't believe we got grades in gym class. I've never used anything I learned in there. All right, I'm standing in front of a room full of strangers. Based on what I learned in gym class, I will throw a red ball at a fat guy."

—Jim Gaffigan

Gym class is another one of those realities that demonstrates that life is unfair. Running a mile is like requiring some birds to fly and other birds to swim.

Did you enjoy gym and physical education classes?

What did you have to wear for you PE classes?

Was there one sport or activity you liked in gym class and others that you didn't?

Do you remember your PE teachers?

Should physical education be a requirement for every student, or should there be alternatives?

Was there one thing you learned in gym class that you still use or remember to this day?

How would you describe the physical education facilities at your school?

Is there a PE teacher that had a positive influence on your thinking about exercise and taking care of your body?

HABITS

"A habit cannot be tossed out the window; it must be coaxed down the stairs a step at a time."

—Mark Twain

"We become what we repeatedly do."

—S. Covey

Habits can be good, and habits can be bad. Through repetition, we can train ourselves to do anything to the point it becomes second nature. It's a choice.

What are some of your habits?

Have you ever consciously tried to develop a good habit or remove a bad one?

What's one habit that you learned from your father or your mother?

Do you have any daily rituals that are required every day?

Do you make your bed and brush your teeth every day?

Was there ever a time where you had the habit of biting your nails or talking with your mouth full?

Do you have nervous habits that are triggered by anxiety?

What's one bad habit you're hoping to get rid of this year?

If there was one behavior you could make into a habit, what would it be?

MEMORIAL DAY

"Mankind must put an end to war before war puts an end to mankind."
—John F. Kennedy

"War is the only game in which both sides lose."
—Walter Scott

Memorial Day is the day we pause to celebrate those men and women who gave the ultimate sacrifice for our freedom. For all those who gave their lives, we take pause because we're grateful.

How has war affected your life?

Do you have family members who have died in military service?

Would you be willing to serve in the military and die for your country?

Have you ever visited a national monument that recognizes and celebrates our fallen war heroes?

How do you usually celebrate Memorial Day?

Do you enjoy watching war movies that celebrate the men and women who gave their lives for our country?

What are some ways we could encourage the next generation to appreciate the sacrifices that men and women have made for our country?

HAIRCUTS

"Hair style is the final tip-off whether or not a woman really knows herself."

—Hubert de Givenchy

"Some of the worst mistakes of my life have been haircuts."

—Jim Morrison

They say the difference between a good haircut and a bad one is two weeks. Some people will spend hundreds to make sure they get a good one immediately.

Do you like getting a haircut?

How often do you get a haircut?

Where do you go to get your haircut, and how much do you pay?

Do you have a "bad haircut" story?

Are you someone who wants a haircut that looks like you didn't have a haircut or someone who wants to make a statement?

Do you give your barber or hairstylist a big tip?

Do you know anyone who makes their living in the field of cosmetology ?

What's the most you've ever paid for a haircut or beauty treatment?

Would you ever wear a wig, dye your hair, or get plugs?

HAPPINESS

"There is only one way to happiness and that is to cease worrying about things which are beyond the power of our will."

—Epictetus

"Happiness is when what you think, what you say, and what you do are in harmony."

—Mahatma Gandhi

Most people can tell you if they are happy or unhappy even if their definition of happiness is unclear. We tend to base our happiness on our circumstances, and those change constantly.

Would you consider yourself to be happy?

Do you think of your childhood as a happy time in your life?

What are the things in life that influence your happiness or unhappiness?

Are you a people pleaser, always trying to make people happy?

Do you believe it is possible to be happy despite our circumstances?

What's one thing that makes you happy that will never change?

What is the trouble with placing our happiness in the possession of things or the love of another person?

What is one thing you could do to increase your happiness?

HAPPY PLACE

"I found my happy place the minute I saw you."

—Sherrilyn Kenyon

"Wherever I am, if I've got a book with me, I have a place I can go and be happy."

—J. K. Rowling

There's nothing better than being in your "happy place." It's the perfect combination of a comfortable space, comfortable clothing, comfortable food, and a comfortable companion.

Where is your "happy place"?

Do you believe a "happy place" has to be a place, or can it just be a frame of mind?

Is your "happy place" something you plan for, or does it just happen?

Are you aware of what constitutes the "happy place" of a friend or family member?

Do you know the meaning and practice of the Danish word *hygge*?

If you were an architect, how would you help people design spaces that would turn into their "happy place"?

When is the next time you expect to be in your "happy place"?

HATRED

"In hatred as in love, we grow like the thing we brood upon. What we loathe, we graft into our very soul."
—Mary Renault

"Nothing brings people together more than mutual hatred."
—Henry Rollins

Hatred is the negative expression of love. Hatred comes from our insecurity and deep fear that something we love is in jeopardy.

Have you ever been able to overcome hatred?

Are you struggling with hate for something or someone right now?

Is there someone in your family who has been controlled by their hatred for a long time?

Do you believe there would ever be a reason that hate could be justified?

Why do you believe there is so much hatred and division in our world today?

What would be a kind way to respond to someone who hates you or something you stand for?

What's one thing you can do today to remove hatred from your life?

HAVING BABIES

"Having a baby is a life-changer. It gives you a whole other perspective on why you wake up every day."

—Taylor Hansen

"A baby is something you carry inside you for nine months, in your arms for three years, and in your heart till the day you die."

—Mary Mason

Having a baby is nothing short of a miracle. From the moment you see that first ultrasound, you're forever changed. You think, "Little one, there's nothing I wouldn't do for you."

———————————

What are your thoughts about having babies?

Did you grow up in a family that celebrated babies?

What do you think is the hardest thing about having a baby?

Have you had difficult conversations with couples who want to have a baby but for whatever reason can't?

How far would you go down the path of infertility treatment to pursue having a child?

Do you believe that some forms of infertility treatment involve too much risk?

Do you want to have a certain number of children?

Have you ever thought about the names of your children and what those names mean?

What would you do if you found out you could never have children?

HEROES

"A hero is someone who has given his or her life to something bigger than oneself."
—Joseph Campbell

"Not every hero wears a mask. Some heroes save the day in the simplest of ways. By just being there for us, or letting us know we're believed in."
—Barry Allen (The Flash)

It doesn't take much to be a hero. Everyday heroes are not known for the powers they have but for the things they surrender. It's the selfless decision to make someone or something more important than yourself.

Do you have a hero?

What are some of your favorite superheroes from cartoons and comic books?

If you could have any superpower, what would you choose?

Was there someone in your life whom you considered a hero who let you down?

Are you someone's hero?

Have you ever met someone who risked their life to save someone else's life?

Have you ever wondered what you would do in a crisis situation where you had to choose to risk your life?

Do you think our culture is overly obsessed with heroes when it should be more concerned with everyday goodness and integrity?

HOBBIES

"My personal hobbies are reading, listening to music, and silence."

—Edith Sitwell

"Happy is the man who can make a living by his hobby."

—George Bernard Shaw

Hobbies provide the pleasure of doing something without the pressure of success. We are free to grow orchids, play the piano, or collect stamps just for the pure joy of it.

Do you have any hobbies?

Have you ever wanted to turn one of your hobbies into a full-time profession?

Did your mom and dad have hobbies when you were young?

Is there someone you know who has a unique hobby?

Is there one hobby that you believe to be a complete waste of time?

Do you believe that hobbies are just another form of escape from life?

Have you ever met someone who was able to quit their day job and make a living with their hobby?

What's one thing you could take up as a hobby that would reduce stress and add value to your life?

HOLIDAYS

"I once wanted to become an atheist, but I gave up—they have no holidays."

—Henny Youngman

"Holi-day: a restoring thing, which, by a blast of magic turns man into himself."

—G. K. Chesterton

Holidays remind us that all days are not the same—we're not on a meaningless treadmill. Holidays unite us with the past, bring celebration to the present, and create expectation for the future.

What's your favorite holiday?

How did you celebrate holidays in your family growing up?

Are holidays stressful for you?

Did you grow up in a community where holidays from different faiths and ethnic traditions were celebrated?

Is there some holiday custom, food, or decoration that you look forward to every year?

Are there any holidays you refuse to celebrate?

Do you have someone in your life who goes overboard when it comes to celebrating holidays?

How do you feel about the commercialization of holidays at the expense of their true meaning?

What's one thing you can do to make the holidays more meaningful?

HOPE

"Hope is a passion for the possible."

—Søren Kierkegaard

"Hope is being able to see that there is light despite all of the darkness."

—Desmond Tutu

Hope is the power to believe even when the facts suggest you shouldn't. It's knowing in your heart that one day good will come.

———————————

Do you consider yourself hopeful?

What is one hope that you have for the future?

Is there one thing for which you have lost all hope?

How do you encourage people in your life to have hope?

Is there someone you know who is hoping for something you don't believe will ever come true?

How do you think our level of hope affects us at the end of our lives?

Do you think that people place too much hope in their jobs, the government, or other things for their security?

What's one thing you hoped for that actually happened?

Is there one area of your life that would benefit from you having more hope?

HOSPITALS

"A hospital bed is a parked taxi with the meter running."

—Groucho Marx

"A hospital is no place to be sick."

—Samuel Goldwyn

On average, one night in a hospital costs just under $4,000, and the average stay is 4.5 days. For some, the hospital bill is more painful than the illness that put them there.

Have you ever been to the hospital?

Do you remember going to visit a family member or loved one in the hospital when you were a child?

What was the name of the hospital where you were born?

Have you ever been rushed to the emergency room?

Is there someone you know who works at a hospital as a doctor, nurse, or in a support position?

What's your experience with hospital food, bed pans, and sponge baths?

What's the longest you or someone you know has stayed in the hospital?

Do you believe hospitals have the best interest of the patient as their priority?

If you were in the hospital, what could someone bring you to encourage you?

HOUSES

"A man's house is his castle."

—James Otis

"It's not the size of the house. It's how much love is inside."

—Martina McBride

A house is a never-ending commitment to maintenance and repair, but a house is also the space where life's most meaningful moments transform it into a home.

———————————————————

Do you own a house?

How do would you describe the house you grew up in?

Did your family live in one house or many houses when you were a child?

How would you describe your dream house?

Is there one house that makes you jealous?

Have you ever considered the option of renting instead of buying a house?

What is the most money you would be willing to spend on a house?

What is one special feature you would like to have in your house?

What do you think makes a house a home?

ICE CREAM

"Someone should open an ice cream shop with flavors like 'Don't Be Sad' and 'You Deserve Better.'"

—Karen Salmansohn

"If you want to make everyone happy, don't be a leader, sell ice cream."

—Steve Jobs

Ice cream is one of those few things in life that is equally enjoyed by everyone. It is no respecter of persons and makes addicts of us all.

———————————————

What's your favorite ice cream?

Did your parents take you out for ice cream at the neighborhood ice cream shop?

Have you ever made your own ice cream at home?

Do you know the difference between gelato, sorbet, sherbet, and ice cream?

What's your favorite brand of ice cream?

Cup or cone?

Do you prefer hand-dipped or soft-serve ice cream?

What the largest amount of ice cream you've ever consumed in one sitting?

If you were to create your own flavor of ice cream, what would it be?

IDEALISM

"Inside every cynical person, there is a disappointed idealist."

—George Carlin

"It is through the idealism of youth that man catches sight of the truth, and in that idealism he possesses a wealth which he must never exchange for anything else."

—Albert Schweitzer

Idealism is often confused with naivete, but to be naive is to be unaware, while the idealist is motivated by the conviction and knowledge that goodness, beauty, and truth actually exist.

Would you consider yourself an idealist?

What are some ideals you think are worth believing in?

Why do you think realists give idealists such a hard time?

Do you know someone who lives out their idealism well?

What would be an example of someone taking their idealism too far?

How do you develop the skills to take idealism and turn it into reality?

In a world obsessed with individualism and personal preference, is it possible there's an ideal we all share?

Would you say that you need to move more toward being an idealist or a realist?

IDENTITY

"Most people are other people. Their thoughts are some-one else's opinions. Their lives a mimicry. Their passions a quotation."

—Oscar Wilde

"The value of identity of course is that so often with it comes purpose."

—Richard Grant

The trouble with identity is that people believe it's their right to dictate to others what defines them. In the end, identity is not the label we give but the life we live.

If you had to explain your identity, what would you say?

How did your parents influence your sense of self and personal identity?

Was there a period of time in your life where your identity was wrapped up in something that no longer matters?

What are some things that society uses to label people and give them a false identity?

Have you ever had your identity stolen?

Where do you believe our identity ultimately comes from?

How do you distinguish who you are from what you do?

Do you think that by answering the questions in this book you can develop a greater sense of identity?

How can you grow in the area of self-acceptance and having a more positive self-image?

194

INDEPENDENCE

"There's no such thing as an independent person."

—Peter Jennings

"What then is freedom? The power to live as one wishes."

—Cicero

Independence is the sweet satisfaction that comes from being smart enough and strong enough to survive on your own. The wise realize early, it never lasts.

Are you independent?

How did your parents teach you to be independent?

Do you believe that independence is an especially American value and that other countries foster interdependence?

How can too much independence be a negative?

When did you feel you made a transition from being dependent on your parents to being independent?

Do you have friends or family members who never "left the nest"?

Do you think that independence is just another word for pride?

In what ways could you be less independent and allow others to help you?

JUNE 10

IDOLATRY

"Idolatry is in a man's own thought, not in the opinion of another."
—John Selden

"Idolatry is when you worship what you should use, and use what you should worship."
—G. K. Chesterton

An idol is basically anything you worship that isn't God. It's not a new concept; it's been around for thousands of years, but now instead of gold statues, people worship gold in other forms.

Are there any people or things you worship?

What are some examples of modern day idols?

Do you believe that *idolatry* is an ancient, outdated term that no longer applies to the 21st century?

Who are the current rock stars and movie stars that have idol status?

Have you ever been someone's idol?

Have you ever been to a country where the people worship statues and figures of their gods?

What's one thing you "idolize" that would be impossible to give up?

Would you find it valuable to ask a friend if they see signs of idolatry in your life?

IMAGINATION

"Imagination is everything. It is the preview of life's coming attractions."

—Albert Einstein

"Imagination should be used, not to escape reality, but to create it."

—Collin Wilson

Imagination is not innately a good thing. Terrible people have imagined many evil things. Imagination is the first step to bringing something into existence, and it is the value of that thing that makes imagination good.

Do you have a strong imagination?

When you were a child, did you have a vivid imagination that introduced you to a land of make-believe?

Were you ever scolded for day-dreaming or drifting off to another place in your mind?

What is one thing in your life that is the product of your imagination?

Is there one thinker, artist, or leader whose imagination for what could be has amazed you?

How do you develop a strong and healthy imagination?

Is there someone in your life who always encourages you to dream and imagine something new?

What's one area of your life that could benefit from a bit of imagination?

IMITATION

"Imitation is the sincerest form of insecurity."
—Polly Bergen

"Children have never been very good at listening to their elders, but they have never failed to imitate them."

—James Baldwin

Imitation is not a bad thing; it all depends on what or whom you choose to imitate. Imitate the masters, the saints, and the pure in heart, and from there, strive to be unique and original.

When was the first time you found yourself imitating someone else?

Were you ever embarrassed by someone making fun of you by imitating something you said or did?

Why is imitation said to be the highest form of praise?

Do you believe that imitating someone else's creative style or technique is cheating?

If someone can make a perfect replica of a masterpiece, wouldn't that be a good thing?

Who is one person you copied and shouldn't have?

Has anyone ever copied you, and how did you respond?

What would be the benefit of finding a successful person and imitating their routine for the next 30 days?

IMPOSTOR SYNDROME

"I still believe that at any time the no-talent police will come and arrest me."

—Mike Meyers

"I have written eleven books, but each time I think, 'uh oh, they're going to find out now. I've run a game on everybody, and they're going to find me out.'"

—Maya Angelou

The trouble with impostor syndrome is that it is fed by our obsession with perfection. Somewhere between competence and perfection we get lost in the disparity between who we are and what we long to be.

Do you struggle with impostor syndrome?

What would it take, or what would you have to accomplish, for impostor syndrome to completely go away?

Is there someone you know who truly is an impostor?

Would it be easier to deal with impostor syndrome if every profession required outside accreditation?

Are there skills or professions so carefully evaluated that any form of impostor syndrome is unwarranted?

What are some of the benefits of struggling with impostor syndrome?

Is there someone in your life who can always say the right things to affirm you and your abilities?

What's one thing you can do today to defy impostor syndrome?

INCITING INCIDENT

"An inciting incident is the event that sets the story in motion."
—Syd Field

"The inciting incident is how you get (characters) to do something. It's the doorway through which they can't return."
—Donald Miller

Some people are fortunate to get kicked out of the nest. Life didn't give them a choice to stay or leave. Other people's inciting incidents were far too subtle, and they are content to live quietly "in the Shire."

Has life presented you with hard choices?

Do you believe there were moments in your life when you had the opportunity to take a huge risk, but took a pass?

Can you think of any stories, novels, or movies where the main character was confronted with an inciting incident?

Do you believe our lives are like a story, with inciting incidents, turning points, villains, and happy endings?

Do you secretly wish that life would present you with an inciting incident, like losing your job?

Could you give examples of inciting incidents in your life?

Was there a person in your life to push you to leave the comfort of the "Shire"?

FATHERS

"One father is more than a hundred schoolmasters."

—George Herbert

"The greatest mark of a father is how he treats his children when no one is looking."

—Dan Pearce

Father's Day is important no matter what your relationship with your father might be. For some it's an opportunity to say thank you; for others, it's an opportunity to forgive.

What do you think makes a good father?

How would you describe your dad?

What's a favorite memory you have of your father?

Do you feel like you need to forgive your dad for something?

How did your dad show love?

What was the greatest lesson you learned from your father?

If God is understood as our father, how does your biological father inform your understanding of God?

What's one thing you and your father disagree on?

How are you most like your father?

INDUSTRIOUSNESS

"There is never a lack of food for the lazy person, nor of work for the industrious.

—Basque Proverb

"The tragedy of bold, forthright, industrious people is that they act so continuously without much thinking, that it becomes dry and empty."

—Brenda Ueland

It's hard to find fault with someone who has an energetic devotion to a task or endeavor. An industrious person may choose the wrong task, but that can be corrected.

Would you consider yourself to be industrious?

Who would you consider to be the hardest working person in your family?

Do you think there is a difference between being industrious and working hard?

Do you believe there is a creature from the animal kingdom that epitomizes the value of being industrious?

Would there be a time in your life where you produced a lot of "smoke" but no "fire"?

How do you motivate yourself to be more industrious?

Was there one teacher or boss who required you to be more industrious to complete a task?

What's one area of your life where you could be more industrious?

INFERIORITY

"Strutting and preening is, in fact, the surest sign of an inferiority complex."

—David Brin

"Many a superior brain is blockaded by inferior thoughts."

—Henry S. Haskins

Feeling inferior is a sure sign of poor perspective. It demonstrates that we see ourselves in a competition based on comparison, and based on what we see, we declare ourselves the loser.

Have you struggled with an inferiority complex?

Has anyone ever modeled inferiority as an expression of humility and servanthood?

How do you see inferiority as destructive?

Do you believe there is a positive way to see our weaknesses without thinking less of ourselves?

How has your pride caused you to see others as inferior?

Is it possible to express superiority and pride without communicating a message to others that they are inferior?

What would you say to encourage a friend who is struggling with inferiority?

What's one perception about inferiority you need to change?

INSECURITY

"Don't let the insecurities of others dull your sparkle. Shine like the star you are born to be."

—Karen Civil

"Relationships fail when people take their own insecurities and project them as their partner's flaws."

—Steve Maraboli

Insecurity is the fear that something in your life is not doing its job to protect you. It may be a lack of physical protection or not having enough money in the bank, but usually it's the fear that someone doesn't like you.

Would you consider yourself to be insecure?

How did your parents provide or fail to provide security in your early years?

Did you experience the typical insecurities of early adolescence and the changes that emerge in junior high?

What are the areas in your life that produce the most anxiety and insecurity?

How do you deal with the insecurities that come from things you can't control?

Who is someone in your life that presents themselves as confident and completely secure?

Do you believe a small amount of insecurity can be a good thing?

What's one thing you can do to remove an insecurity in your life?

JUSTICE

"The dead cannot cry out for justice. It is a duty of the living to do so for them."

—Lois McMaster Bujold

"Justice consists not in being neutral between right and wrong but in finding out the right and upholding it, wherever found, against the wrong."

—Theodore Roosevelt

Today is Juneteenth, the holiday that celebrates the emancipation of slaves in America. It's a day that celebrates justice, and a very important triumph of good over evil in this country.

Do you believe most people share a clear definition of justice?

Have you ever been treated unjustly?

Do you feel that the justice system of your government has integrity and is effective?

What do you believe our country can do to address issues of racism, prejudice, and injustice?

Are you someone who tends to lean toward the rules and justice, or do you lean more toward forgiveness and grace?

How have you seen justice expressed this past year?

In what way can you help promote a better expression of justice in your life and community?

INTROVERTS

"Solitude matters, and for some people, it's the air they breathe."
—Susan Cain

"That's the thing about introverts; we wear our chaos on the inside where no one can see it."
—Michaela Chung

Let's face it, society doesn't celebrate introverts like it does extroverts. We make stars out of people who love to perform and be up front. For introverts, we "coach" them to come out of their shell.

Are you an introvert?

Why do you think introverts aren't more celebrated?

How many people in your family are introverts and how many are extroverts?

Have you ever seen an introvert be shamed for wanting to be alone?

How could our education system be modified to promote and celebrate introverts?

What's one thing introverts could do to help the rest of the world understand and accept them?

Do you feel that our goal should be to merge our introverted/extrovertedness toward the middle?

What would be a fun way to celebrate an introvert in your life?

JEALOUSY

"As iron is eaten away by rust, so the envious are consumed by their own passion.

—Antisthenes

"There is no greater glory than love, nor any greater punishment than jealousy."

—Lope de Vega

Jealousy reveals the depth of low self-esteem. It makes us believe that we are not as lovable, as gifted, as deserving, or as blessed as someone else.

Do you struggle with jealousy?

Is there one thing you wish you had that you've observed someone else enjoying?

When was the first time you can remember being jealous?

Do you know someone who does things or buys things just to make other people jealous?

In what area of your life are you completely content?

What is the easiest way to make you jealous: is it relationships, travel, beauty, or possessions?

Do you believe couples can do things to protect their relationships from jealousy?

What's one way you can grow in your contentment and be grateful for what you have?

JOURNALING

"I can shake off everything as I write; my sorrow disappears, my courage is reborn."

—Anne Frank

"I write because I don't know what I think until I read what I say."

—Flannery O'Connor

A journal is a valuable resource for anyone seeking to live an intentional life. A journal makes your thoughts tangible, records your life history, and provides a place for ideas to grow, wait, and percolate.

Do you practice journaling?

Have any of your friends or family members demonstrated a consistent commitment to using a journal?

In what ways do you believe a journal might benefit your life now and influence your future?

Have you ever written something deeply personal only to read it later and quickly destroy it?

Have you ever been guilty of reading someone else's journal or wishing you could?

What information would you think to be most helpful to record in a personal diary or journal?

Do you think a sketchbook or field book for recording data could be just as valuable as a traditional journal?

What would it take for you to buy a journal this year and faithfully make entries every day?

JUNIOR HIGH

"If there is hell, it was modeled after Junior High School."

—Lewis Black

"When I feel confused or depressed, I remember back to junior high and I silently repeat, 'This, too, shall pass.'"

—Josh Groban

Junior high is one of life's perfect storms. Your body betrays you, your friends humiliate you, and the only thing you can do is wait it out and hope you survive.

———————————————————————

How would you describe your junior high years?

Do you have one particularly embarrassing moment from junior high?

How were the inevitable facts of puberty explained to you?

Was there a parent, teacher, coach, or friend that was encouraging to you during junior high?

What do you think is one thing parents or teachers could do to make those awkward years more tolerable?

Do you feel that your experience with puberty was easier or harder than most?

What were your favorite sports, hobbies, or things to do in junior high school?

What's one thing you would say to your junior high self that would have made the most difference?

JUNK FOOD

"There's no such thing as junk food. There's junk and there's food."

—Mark Hyman

"If you put junk food in your body, your body will turn to junk."

—Goldie Hawn

At what point should junk food be required to have a warning from the surgeon general like cigarettes? The scientific evidence clearly condemns it, but somehow we still feel like we're giving ourselves a treat.

Are you prone to eat junk food?

What's one thing you ate as a child that you wouldn't even think about eating today?

What's your biggest temptation when it comes to junk food?

Do you take the time to read the label and the ingredients that go into the processed foods you eat?

What's the one thing you could remove from your diet that would make the biggest difference?

Are there any healthy foods that you enjoy as much or more than junk food?

If we visited your kitchen, pantry, and refrigerator, what would we find inside?

Are you craving a certain junk food right now?

KEEPING SECRETS

"Three may keep a secret, if two of them are dead."

—Benjamin Franklin

"To keep your secret is wisdom; but to expect others to keep it is folly."

—Samuel Johnson

To keep a secret is to protect a relationship. Prove that you can be trusted, for one day you may need to share a secret too.

Are you able to keep a secret?

Has anyone ever betrayed your trust by sharing your secret with someone else?

Have you ever told someone a secret you should have kept to yourself?

Who is someone in your life that you can trust with your deepest, darkest secrets?

Do you believe there are things about ourselves that we should never tell to anyone?

Have you ever kept a personal matter a secret for a long period of time?

Is there some secret you're dying to share with someone?

How confident are your friends and family that you can keep their secrets?

KINDERGARTEN

"All I really need to know... I learned in kindergarten."

—Robert Fulghum

"If we learned everything there is to know in kindergarten, it was promptly drummed out of us in first grade."

—Peter McWilliams

Kindergarten in German is the combination of the words children and garden. Kindergarten should be a place you love to be—a place where you grow.

Did you have a positive experience in kindergarten?

What was your kindergarten teacher's name, and what were they like?

What's one of your most lasting memories from kindergarten?

Do you still maintain contact with anyone from your kindergarten class?

What do you remember about your kindergarten classroom?

Did you go kindergarten a full day or half day?

What was your most favorite activity in kindergarten?

How do you think kindergarten has changed since you were a child?

JUNE 27

KINDNESS

"There are three ways to ultimate success. The first way is to be kind. The second way is to be kind. The third way is to be kind."
—Mister Rogers

"There's no such things as a small act of kindness. Every act creates a ripple with no logical end."
—Scott Adams

Kindness is always a good idea. Even when people are cruel, respond with kindness. It will confuse them to death, which is what we mean when we say, "Kill them with kindness."

Do you consider yourself to be kind?

Who was kind to you when you were young?

Has anyone ever been especially unkind to you?

Have you ever asked someone to forgive you for being unkind?

What's the best way for someone to impress you with their kindness?

What are the things that keep us from being kind to one another?

Do you think it's possible for you to respond to cruelty with kindness?

What is one simple, random act of kindness you could perform today?

JUNE 28

KISSING

"A kiss is a lovely trick designed by nature to stop speech when words become superfluous."

—Ingrid Bergman

"It is the passion that is in a kiss that gives to it its sweetness; it is the affection in a kiss that sanctifies it."

—Christian Nestell Bovee

Kissing is pure proof that life and love are not completely rational. Why would any germ-conscious individual engage in such a wet and sloppy exchange?

Would you consider yourself a good kisser?

When was your first romantic kiss?

Did you ever practice kissing?

What makes something as odd as pressing your lips against someone else's so amazing?

In real life, the movies, or the stage, what would you say was the most romantic kiss of all time?

Do you think a hug can be just as romantic as a kiss?

Have you been to a country where people greet each other with a kiss?

When was the last time you were kissed?

How do you plan to keep kissing a meaningful practice in your life well into old age?

LAZINESS

"Laziness is nothing more than the habit of resting before you get tired."
—Jules Renard

"There is no such thing as a lazy person; he is either sick or uninspired."
—Zig Ziglar

People you might consider lazy are not tired; they've just given up trying. If life doesn't improve from hard work and effort, it's logical to pursue the same result by taking a nap.

Are you lazy?

How do you motivate yourself to keep going when you don't feel like it?

What are the factors that contribute to your laziness?

Do you think laziness has produced more efficient ways of doing things without all the work?

Who is the hardest working person you know? The laziest?

What's one thing you would do more often if you knew you would get better results?

Do you believe that some cultures or some parts of the world are unfairly judged as lazy?

What's one thing you can do today to defeat laziness?

JUNE 30

LEADERSHIP

"The greatest leader is not necessarily the one who does the greatest things. He is the one that gets the people to do the greatest things."

—Ronald Reagan

"If your actions inspire others to dream more, learn more, do more, and become more, you are a leader."

—John Quincy Adams

Leadership should not be something we pursue but something we earn. Leaders with charisma are suspect, but those who lead by serving never make you doubt.

———————————————————

Would you consider yourself a leader?

Would your friends, family, and colleagues consider you a leader?

What would you say are the most important qualities of a good leader?

Who was the best leader you ever followed?

Why do you think there are so many books, conferences, and courses on leadership?

Do you think leadership is a natural ability that some people are just born with?

What's the best resource for developing leadership?

How can you develop leadership skills that will serve others and get more things done?

LEARNING

"Anyone who stops learning is old, whether at twenty or eighty. Anyone who keeps learning stays young."

—Henry Ford

"Tell me and I forget. Teach me and I remember. Involve me and I learn."

—Benjamin Franklin

Learn to love learning with all your heart. It will lead to an extraordinary life with more possibilities than you ever imagined. It will also lead you to the knowledge you will need to solve problems along the way.

———————————————

How would you describe your attitude toward learning?

Who was the first person that showed you learning could be fun?

Do you have a fond memory of learning to do something for the first time?

Was there a time when learning was hard and painful?

Are you currently trying to learn something on your own through tutorials, a book, or an online course?

Do you know your learning style or how you learn best?

What's something you learned the hard way?

What's one thing you would like to learn in the next year?

LEARNING TO READ

"To learn to read is to light a fire; every syllable that is spelled out is a spark."
—Victor Hugo

"Reading is the gateway skill that makes all other learning possible."
—Barack Obama

Learning to read is like learning to walk. You can survive without it, but you won't get very far. And that's sad, but what's worse is you'll never know the places you could've gone and the things you could've done.

How would you describe your experience of learning to read?

Who was the person who encouraged you the most to learn to read?

Was there one book or story that sparked your desire to read?

Did your teacher require you to read out loud in class, and was that embarrassing?

What kinds of books are you drawn to—non-fiction or fiction?

Do you believe that videos and audio books are changing the way we think about reading?

What's the best reading experience you've ever had?

LEARNING TO SWIM

"A man is not learned until he can read, write, and swim."

—Plato

"You can't learn to swim on a piano bench."

—Milton H. Erickson

Learning to swim might save your life someday, but in the meantime, it's a great, low-impact workout that burns a lot of calories. It's also a great way to cool off and have some fun.

How would you describe your experience of learning to swim?

Who was the person who encouraged you the most to learn to swim?

Was there one day at the pool, lake, or beach where it all just clicked and you loved swimming?

Did you ever take a formal swimming class at your school or local pool?

Have you ever had a scary moment where you thought you were going to drown?

Do you know how to swim using different strokes, like freestyle, breast stroke, back stroke, and the butterfly?

Many schools require their students to take swimming classes. Do you believe that learning to swim should be required?

FOURTH OF JULY

"We must be free, not because we claim freedom, but because we practice it."
—William Faulkner

"We on this continent should never forget that men first crossed the Atlantic not to find soil in their ploughs but to secure liberty for their souls."
—Robert J. McCracken

Today is Independence Day in America. It's hard to imagine what life was like in this country before 1776. We can say we appreciate our freedom, but how do we come to cherish it if it's all we've ever known?

———————————————

What are you doing today to celebrate your freedom?

How did your family celebrate the Fourth of July or your country's independence day?

How have you celebrated this holiday over the years: a picnic, fireworks, and parades?

What do you think about fireworks as a form of celebration?

Would you consider yourself to be patriotic? Do you wear red, white, and blue, and fly the flag?

What are some ways that we can continue to value and commemorate our liberty and freedom as a country?

How would you rate your knowledge of the history of the American Revolution?

LIES

"I am not upset that you lied to me; I'm upset that from now on I can't believe you."

—Friedrich Nietzsche

"We lie the loudest when we lie to ourselves."

—Eric Hoffer

If the truth sets us free, then lies produce prisons. Prisons are lonely places filled with lonely people, and when you lie to yourself, that's the loneliest place on the earth.

———————————

When are you most tempted to tell a lie?

Do you believe that it's okay to tell "white lies"?

What was the most devastating lie anyone has ever told you?

Have you ever been able to completely trust someone after they told you a lie?

What do you believe are some pervasive lies that have been accepted as truth in society?

Are you someone who tends to believe that you are being told the truth?

What's one lie you told that you regret to this day?

Is there a lie or untruth in your life that needs to be resolved or reconciled?

LIFE AT AGE 07

"When my daughter was about seven years old, she asked me one day what I did at work. I told her I worked at a college —that my job was to teach people to draw. She stared at me, incredulous, and said, "You mean they forget?"

—Howard Ikemoto

"I thought I needed a hug, but I really need pancakes."

—Anonymous, 7 years old

<u>28 Up</u> is the title of a famous documentary. The film interviewed the same children at age 7, 14, 21, and 28. The film is based on Aristotle's statement "Give me a child until he is seven, and I will show you the man."

———————————————

How would you describe your life at age seven?

What are some traits and qualities you had at seven that still characterize you today?

Who was the most influential person in your life at age seven?

Can you describe where you lived, your house, your room, your neighborhood at age seven?

What were some of your greatest fears at this age?

What's one memory from age seven that you'll never forget?

Who were your best friends at age seven?

If you could relive your life at seven, what would you repeat and what would you change?

LIFE AT AGE 14

"When it comes to age, I just feel like puberty is, like, the most horrible time of anyone's life."

—Sam Smith

"Our culture is definitely the eighth grade. It's run by eighth-grade boys, and the way these boys show a girl they like her is by humiliating her and making her cry."

—Merrill Markoe

In 1843, Hans Christian Andersen wrote "The Ugly Duckling," the story of an ugly baby duck's transformation into a beautiful adult swan. It should be required reading for everyone in junior high.

How would you describe your life at age 14?

It may not have been at age 14, but did you go through an awkward, "ugly duckling" stage?

Who was the most influential person in your life at age 14?

Can you describe where you lived, your house, your room, your neighborhood at age 14?

What were some of your greatest fears at this age?

What's one memory from age 14 that you'll never forget?

Who were your best friends at age 14?

If you could relive your life at 14, what would you repeat and what would you change?

LIFE AT AGE 21

"When you turn 21, you can legally do all the things you've already been doing since you were 15."

—Earl Dibbles, Jr.

"Age 21-23... The only stage in your life where neither you can behave like an adult nor can you roam around like a teenager."

—Sudip Kumar Roy

Turning 21 is a rite of passage. It's the time when adults start taking you seriously. Your plans for your life, what you believe, your career, who you'll marry—they are no longer dreams and fantasy; it's your life.

———————————————

How would you describe your life at age 21?

Why do think 21 is the age we have chosen as the portal for adulthood? Why not 18 or 16?

Who was the most influential person in your life at age 21?

Can you describe where you lived, your house, your room, your neighborhood at age 21?

What were some of your greatest fears at this age?

What's one memory from age 21 that you'll never forget?

Who were your best friends at age 21?

If you could relive your life at 21, what would you repeat and what would you change?

LIFE AT AGE 28

"At age 18 you can say I'm poor, but at age 28 you shouldn't say I'm poor."

—Unknown

"What screws us up most in life is the picture in our head of how it's supposed to be."

—Jeremy Binns

Age 28 is one of life's mile markers. Society steps back and says, "Okay, you've had enough time to prove yourself. Are you successful? Are you married? It's the anxiety of a ten-year high school reunion.

How would you describe, or like to describe, your life at age 28?

What are (or were) some of your goals to achieve or dreams you have (or had) for you life at age 28?

Are you someone who wanted to get settled down by the age of 28?

Do you feel that society puts too much pressure on young people to be successful by a certain age?

Who's the most successful person you know in their twenties?

How could we do a better job celebrating and encouraging the "late bloomers" in our lives?

What's one thing you want to make sure happens (or you're glad happened) by age 28?

LIFE VERSE

"A memorized scripture becomes an enduring friend that does not weaken with the passage of time."

—Richard G. Scott

"I love quotations because it is a joy to find thoughts one might have, beautifully expressed with much authority by someone recognized wiser than oneself."
—Marlene Dietrich

A life verse, slogan, or mantra summarizes the central truth or theme of your life. Memorize and repeat these words of truth, and they will define your life's purpose; they will motivate you and keep your life on course.

What is your life verse, or the words you live by?

Have you ever memorized Bible verses, famous quotes, or wise sayings?

Would you say that your life is focused and has a clear purpose and theme?

Were there verses, phrases, or sayings that were used in your family to promote virtues or values?

What's the worst piece of conventional wisdom that people share without thinking?

Do you believe there are virtues and values in life that are universal and timeless?

What is your opinion about the Bible as a source of truth and instruction?

LISTENING

"One of the most sincere forms of respect is actually listening to what another has to say."

—Bryant H. McGill

"The biggest communication problem is we do not listen to understand. We listen to reply."

—Stephen R. Covey

Many people confuse listening with waiting for their turn to speak. Listening isn't passive patience; it's aggressive, active interest in someone else.

———————————————

How would you describe your listening skills?

Who is someone who is a good listener?

When was the last time you caught yourself nodding your head while someone was talking but didn't hear a word?

Do you believe we are losing our ability to listen because of all the "digital noise" in our lives?

Who is someone in your life that you find it's easy to listen to?

Do you believe that people who don't have friends or can't get dates just lack the ability to listen?

Have you ever been in a situation where you were asked to put down your phone, remove all distractions, and engage with someone or a group of people?

Who is one person you should listen to more intently?

LONG SUFFERING

"Wisdom comes alone through suffering."

—Aeschylus

"Pain and suffering are always inevitable for a large intelligence and a deep heart. The really great men must, I think, have a great sadness on earth."

—Fyodor Dostoevsky

Suffering is relative. For most of us, suffering means no air conditioning, cold soup, or waiting in line. We would do well to place life's minor irritations in perspective and consider what it means to truly suffer.

———————————————————

Was there a time in your life when you experienced true suffering?

Who is the most long-suffering person you know?

Have you ever considered how you might respond to being homeless, without food, or deathly ill?

How does someone cope with constant and prolonged suffering?

Is there someone you know who is constantly complaining about the pain and suffering in their life?

How do you determine the difference between someone who is easily irritated and genuine suffering?

Have you ever willingly suffered or sacrificed for the benefit of someone else?

LOSING

"You are not defeated when you lose. You are defeated when you quit."

—Paulo Coelho

"Losing is only temporary and not encompassing. You must simply study it, learn from it, and try hard not to lose the same way again. Then you must have the self-control to forget about it."

—John Wooden

Athletic competition provides a great way to put losing in perspective—it teaches us to respond, regroup, and grow. Losing in life is not so easy, but you still have the opportunity to respond, regroup, and grow.

How would you describe your ability to deal with losing?

Did you play board games as a child, and how did you respond when you lost?

Was there a time when you were a poor loser?

Who do you know is a gracious loser? A terrible loser?

Is there one area in your life where you were a loser but decided to learn from your mistakes and win?

Were you ever part of a team that competed for a prize, trophy, or championship?

What's one area of your life where you are currently experiencing defeat but could turn it around?

LOST

"Being lost is worth the being found."
—Neil Diamond

"Some beautiful paths can't be discovered without getting lost."
—Erol Ozan

Being lost is one of those ideas that works both in the physical world and the abstract. Someone can have a great sense of direction and be "lost" without purpose; others need a GPS for every turn but know exactly where they're going.

How would describe your physical sense of direction?

How has GPS changed your life?

As a child were you ever lost or separated for a time from your family?

J.R.R Tolkien wrote, "Not all those who wander are lost." Have you ever purposefully set out on a journey without a clear destination?

How is being physically lost a good analogy for not having a clear purpose or plan for your life?

Do you believe that it's all that bad to be wandering in life without purpose, or is that how we find our way?

If you can "get lost" in life, then what do you believe are life's maps, compasses, and GPS devices?

LOST FRIENDSHIP

"The loss of a friend is like that of a limb; time may heal the anguish of the wound, but the loss cannot be repaired."

—Robert Southey

"You don't lose friends, because real friends can never be lost. You lose people masquerading as friends, and you're better for it."

—Mandy Hale

True friendship is rare, and you are truly blessed if you have but a few lifelong friends. The older you get, the more you realize it's the quality, not the quantity, and it's hard not to lose some friends along the way.

What do you believe causes friendships to end?

Do you remember losing a friendship as a child?

What friendship would be the most painful to lose?

Do you have any friendships that were lost for awhile but are now significant again?

Were there some friendships in your life that were bad influences on your life?

What do think makes some friendships long-lasting?

Is there a friendship you need to discontinue?

Is there a friendship you need to renew or rescue?

LOVE LANGUAGES

"Sometimes you love people in a language they cannot understand."

—Unknown

"The five love languages are words of affirmation, quality time, receiving gifts, acts of service, and physical touch."

—Gary Chapman

Marriage counselors will tell you that what it means to be loved is not the same for everyone. It's fascinating to think, but it may be more loving to pick your underwear off the floor than to buy a dozen roses.

What do you think about the theory that people experience love in different ways?

Have you ever had someone try to do something loving for you but it had no effect on you?

What was the most loving thing that anyone has ever done for you?

Which of the five love languages above would be your favorite? Do you speak and understand them all?

Is there someone you love who only feels loved through a specific expression or activity?

Why do you think it's important to love a person the way they feel loved, as opposed to loving them the way you do?

Relationships take a lot of work. Are you someone who naturally enjoys the hard work of a relationship?

LOVE IT, BUT...

"Anything worth doing is worth doing poorly at first."

—Brian Tracy

"People are going to judge you anyway, so you might as well do what you want."

—Taylor Swift

How sad to think of the thousands, if not millions, of people who don't sing, dance, or play the piano because they didn't think they were good enough. If you love to do something, give yourself permission to do it poorly.

What's something you love to do but aren't very good at?

Have you ever stopped doing something you love because someone said you weren't very good at it?

Should we tell people the truth so that they don't live deluded lives, convinced they are good at something when they're not?

Do you believe that you are good at something, and perhaps a bit deceived by your own opinion?

Do you think the real issue is being self-aware, that you can be bad at something just as long as you know you are?

What is something you could be doing for fun and pleasure right now that your standards for quality prohibit?

How can we encourage people to pursue things based on their passion and motives and not on their skill?

LOYALTY

"Loyalty isn't grey. It's black and white. You're either loyal completely, or not loyal at all."

—Sharnay

"Some people aren't loyal to you; they are loyal to their need of you. Once their needs change, so does their loyalty."

—Unknown

Someone who is loyal is like an anchor, a strong foundation, or mighty fortress. We know life is unpredictable, but those who are loyal help us weather any storm.

How would you describe yourself when it comes to being loyal?

Who do you believe has been the most constant and loyal person in your life?

When was a time in your life where you felt betrayed by a person you thought was loyal to you?

What do you think it means to be "loyal to a fault"?

Is loyalty an essential requirement of citizenship, marriage, employment, or membership?

Do you know someone who presents themselves as loyal when you know they aren't?

In what areas or relationships in your life do you need to be loyal?

LUCK

"I'm a greater believer in luck, and I find the harder I work the more I have it."

—Thomas Jefferson

"The only good luck many great men ever had was being born with the ability and determination to overcome bad luck."

—Channing Pollock

Some people call it luck, some call it good fortune, and others call it providence. Whatever you call it, you know it was something good, and you can't take any credit for it, other than being there to receive it.

Would you consider yourself to be lucky?

Do you believe in luck, or do you call it something else?

Do you believe that some people get more breaks in life than others?

Have you ever won a raffle, lottery, or contest where the winner was chosen at random?

Who is the luckiest person you know? Unluckiest?

Do you believe the events of our lives are just random, or are they part of a divine plan?

What do you think about the lottery and spending money on the chance of getting rich?

How are you preparing now so you will be ready when that lucky break presents itself?

JULY 20

LUST

*"Lust is a poor, weak, whimpering, whispering thing
compared with that richness and energy of desire which will
arise when lust has been killed."*

—C. S. Lewis

"The desire of love is to give. The desire of lust is to take."

—Unknown

Lust has ruined many lives. It's a fantasy that begins
with the eyes, goes to the brain, which then produces
an addictive drug call dopamine. Lust is a self-centered,
destructive addiction to sexual fantasy and pleasure,
and we need to talk about it.

How have you experienced the destructive qualities of lust?

How did you parents or family teach you about the realities
and negative effects of lust and pornography?

Have you ever been addicted to pornography?

Some would argue that lust is a harmless, invisible act of the
mind and there is no victim. Do you agree?

Why do you think lust is so powerful, to the point where
presidents, CEO's, and world leaders have lost everything?

What safeguards have you put in place to keep lust out of
your life?

How do you believe couples can be open, transparent, and
accountable to each other on this issue?

JULY 21

LUXURY

"Give me the luxuries of life and I will willingly do without the necessities."
—Frank Lloyd Wright

"Real luxury is understanding quality, and having the time to enjoy it."
—G. Bruce Boyer

Some might defend the pursuit of luxury under the pretense of quality, but luxury is based not on pragmatics but status. Luxury produces pleasure, but more importantly, it's the calling card of the elite.

What are some things you consider to be a luxury?

Are you currently saving or strategizing to purchase a luxury item or experience?

Do you believe most people who pursue luxury items are more concerned with status than quality?

Do you believe that luxury items should be taxed at a higher percentage?

Is there one luxury brand that you're obsessed with?

What's one luxury item that makes absolutely no sense to you?

Is pursuing luxury an issue that's clearly right or wrong?

What's one thing you consider to be luxurious that does not have societal status connected to it?

PARENTING

"Too many parents make life hard for their children by trying, too zealously, to make it easy for them."
—Geothe

"Making the decision to have a child—it is momentous. It is to decide forever to have your heart go walking around outside your body."
—Elizabeth Stone

Parenting unites all parents together like no other challenge in life. Your child has the power to bring you great joy or great sorrow, and it all rests on your ability to make wise yes and no decisions.

How would you describe your parents and their parenting style?

How is your philosophy of being a parent different than your parents' philosophy?

Is there someone that you believe models good parenting skills?

How do you feel about being strict with children, enforcing discipline, or corporal punishment?

Do you think you would be (are) a "tiger mom" or "helicopter parent"?

What do you believe is the single, biggest mistake that parents make today?

What would happen if our schools provided courses on parenting?

MAKING

"The 'maker movement' is about moving from consumption to creation and turning knowledge into action."

—Laura Fleming

"The YouTube video maker gets more out of making a video than you get out of watching it."

—Seth Godin

The maker movement began with a passion to celebrate our human desire to make things. At it's core is a desire to make resources available at the grassroots level, rejecting mass production for meaning-based making.

Do you like to make things?

What's your earliest memory of making a craft, a meal, an invention?

Is there someone in your life who makes their living as a self-employed maker or creative?

Is there a small brand or maker-based product that you wholeheartedly support and love?

If you could make a living from making something, what would you make and what would your brand look like?

Are you willing to pay more for something that is made by hand, produced locally, or crafted by someone you know?

What are the benefits of knowing where products come from and who was responsible for making them?

MARRIAGE

"Happy is the man who finds a true friend, and far happier is he who finds that true friend is his wife."

—Franz Schubert

"A perfect marriage is just two imperfect people who refuse to give up on each other."

—Kate Stewart

Marriage is a sacred covenant. Good marriages are based on the promise, not on the person. People and circumstances may change, but our vows remain.

———————————————————

Why do you think so many marriages fail?

Did your parents have a happy, healthy marriage?

How would you characterize your marriage (or hope for a future marriage)?

What would you say are the most important distinctions between marriages that last and those that don't?

How do you feel about living together before marriage, open marriage, or pre-nups?

Do you believe it's important to get married in a church?

What's your feeling about pre-marital counseling?

What do you think are the benefits of being married, and what are its biggest challenges?

MATHEMATICS

"Math is the only place where truth and beauty mean the same thing."

—Danica McKellar

"The beauty of mathematics only shows itself to more patient followers."

—Maryam Mirzakhani

In 2016, the film *The Man Who Knew Infinity* was released. It's the story of a man from India who shocked the world with his mathematical genius. His life and work celebrate mathematics as beautiful and divine.

How were you introduced to mathematics, and did you enjoy the encounter?

What was your last mathematics class?

Did you have a math teacher that made you appreciate math or just the opposite?

Other than simple addition, subtraction, multiplication, and division, do you use any advanced math skills in your life?

Could you explain the difference between algebra, geometry, trigonometry, and calculus?

Who is the most talented mathematician you know?

Do you use a calculator on a regular basis?

How would you motivate a grade school student to appreciate math and/or pursue a career that requires math skills?

MEDIOCRITY

"Jealousy is the tribute mediocrity pays to genius."

—Fulton J. Sheen

"Mediocrity never goes away, but neither, I hope, do those who are willing to challenge it."

—Milos Forman

Statistically speaking, most people are mediocre at what they do, but being in the majority shouldn't give us cause to stop trying; nor should it send us into depression.

Would you consider yourself to be mediocre in any way?

How did your parents confront mediocrity and complacency?

Have you come to a place in your life where you are content with the status quo?

How can you continue to pursue excellence if you know there's little chance of obtaining it?

Do you think it's acceptable to be content with mediocrity as long as you can sustain an acceptable quality of life?

Are you concerned that someone in your life has settled for results that are far too low?

Have you ever considered the thought that this is as good as it gets?

What's one thing you can do to fight mediocrity this week?

MEDITATION

"The practice of meditation can reveal to you more of your mental capacity."
—Betty Buckley

"Eastern meditation is an attempt to empty the mind; Christian meditation is an attempt to fill the mind. The two ideas are quite different."
—Richard J. Foster

Meditation is a practice that pursues mental clarity, emotional calm, and stable being. The argument is whether one should pursue the fruits of meditation by emptying the mind or by filling it.

Do you have a meditation practice?

How would you define the practice of meditation to someone?

Have you ever gone away on a spiritual retreat or dedicated several hours for personal reflection and contemplation?

Do you have a morning ritual that includes time for quiet, soulful meditation?

Do you have a spiritual leader, guide, pastor, or mentor?

Is there a passage of Scripture or a spiritual resource that has been helpful to you?

Do you believe that people are looking for a deeper spiritual connection in their lives?

What are some benefits that come from deciding to slow down and be quiet without distraction?

MEMORIZATION

"Students are rewarded for memorization, not imagination and resourcefulness."
—Sugata Mitra

"Memorization isn't anti-creativity or anti-innovation; it is the foundation of that process."
—Blake Harvard

The brain isn't a muscle, but it does seem to increase its potential based on the demands we give it. A good memory may be replaced by a fast Internet connection, but a good mind still needs to be filled with good things.

———————————————

Would you consider yourself to have a good memory?

Were you ever required to memorize a massive amount of information for a school project or performance?

Are there some things you memorized as a child that you can still recall and recite today?

Some educators would say that facts and dates represent inert knowledge. If so, what would be some good things to memorize?

Can you name all the states and their capitals?

How hard is it for you to remember someone's name?

Is it easier for you to remember numbers or words?

What are some tricks or mnemonic devices you use to remember important things?

MEN

"Masculinity is not something given to you but something you gain. And you gain it by winning small battles with honor."

—Norman Mailer

"I prefer men to boys. To clear it up, it's not about an older or younger thing. It's a mindset, not age. There are 18-year-old men out there and there are 40-year-old boys."

—Keri Hilson

In 2004, Robert Bly wrote the book *Iron John: A Book About Men* where he mourned the disappearance of male initiation and male rites of passage in our culture. There's value in pursuing masculinity and manhood.

In your opinion, what does it mean to be a man?

How would you say men are different than women?

Who would you say are some positive role models of masculinity in the world today?

Do you believe that boys are being discouraged to pursue traditional expressions of masculinity?

What is one thing that would help women better understand men?

Have divorce and absent fathers contributed to the decline of male initiation?

What is one thing you can do to help yourself or someone else be a better man this week?

FRIENDSHIP

"Friends are the siblings God never gave us."

—Mencius

"The only way to have a friend is to be one."

—Ralph Waldo Emerson

Friendship comes in many forms. It may be a recent relationship based on a mutual interest in fly fishing or a 75-year-old bond formed in kindergarten. Whatever it is, science says friendship will help you live longer.

Would you consider yourself to be a good friend?

What is the basis for your most important friendships?

Did your parents have deep friendships that influenced your family and your understanding of friendship?

Who would you consider to be your best friend?

Why do you think it's easier to make friendship when you're young and it gets progressively more difficult?

Have you ever had a significant friendship with someone who wasn't the same age?

Have you ever had a purely platonic friendship with someone of the opposite sex?

In what ways could you be a better friend to the people you care about most?

MENTORS

"A mentor is someone who sees more talent and ability within you than you see in yourself and helps bring it out of you."

—Bob Proctor

"One of the greatest values of mentors is the ability to see ahead what others cannot see and to help them navigate a course to their destination."

—John C. Maxwell

True mentors are rare. They are men and women who are secure and accomplished enough to sacrifice their own time for the benefit of someone else. They value the hope and promise of a future you.

Do you have a mentor?

Have you ever considered being a mentor to someone else?

What are the major factors that make someone a good mentor?

Was there ever a time in your life when you could have used a good mentor but you had to figure it out for yourself?

Have you ever participated in a boys or girls club to help kids grow and develop strong life skills?

Do you believe it's important to have more than one mentor—one personal, one professional?

What's one area of your life that could benefit from the wisdom and advice of a mentor or life coach?

MILESTONES

"Small milestones are the stepping stones of big dreams."

—Anne Grace

"People throw stones at you, and you convert them into milestones."

—Sachin Tendulkar

Always remember to celebrate moments of accomplishment in your life. Take a photograph or plant a tree. Do something tangible, so you can look back and say, "I really did that, and so can you!"

What do you believe are some of life's milestones?

How did your family celebrate the major milestones and accomplishments in your life?

Is there one major milestone or accomplishment in your life that is especially important to you?

Do you have a photograph, a trophy, or some other physical artifact that marks a milestone for you?

What would you say to someone who sees the celebration of milestones as an expression of pride?

Is there someone in your life who would benefit from you taking the time to celebrate what they've accomplished?

What do you believe is one of life's overlooked milestones?

What will be the next major milestone in your life?

MONEY

"Don't think money does everything or you are going to end up doing everything for money."

—Voltaire

"The money you make is a symbol of the value you create."

—Idowu Koyenikan

Learn to master the role of money in your life. Your happiness depends on the significance it holds. Make sure it does not consume you either by its abundance or its absence.

Do you believe you have enough money?

How did your parents demonstrate the role of money in your family?

Are you a saver or a spender?

Do you want to be rich?

Have you ever been foolish in the way that you've managed your money?

Who is someone in your life who has been very wise with their money?

How much money is enough money for you?

What's one piece of advice about money that you would pass along to someone else?

How much time do you spend thinking about your finances?

MOMENTS

"We do not remember days; we remember moments."

—Cesare Pavese

"Sometimes you will never know the value of a moment until it becomes a memory."

—Dr. Seuss

Most of life is uneventful, some might even say mundane, but every now and then you experience a "moment." You fall in love; beauty takes your breath away; you witness a miracle.

What is one moment you will never forget?

Did you ever witness a moment in someone else's life that had great impact on them and also on you?

Has something or someone ever taken your breath away?

Do you believe it's possible to make an unforgettable moment?

What is the worst moment you've ever experienced?

Have you ever had a moment you can't explain or an encounter with something beyond the physical world?

Is there a moment in your future that you're looking forward to with great anticipation?

What's one thing we can do to make sure that we don't miss life's most beautiful moments?

MORNING PERSON

"I never knew a man come to greatness or eminence who lay abed late in the morning."

—Jonathan Swift

"I'm not a morning person. I drink coffee because morning people exist, and they keep trying to talk to me."

—Unknown

It's hard not to be biased in praise of morning people. They willingly leave the warmth, safety, and comfort of bed in exchange for the hopeful possibilities of a new day.

What do you think of morning people?

Were your parents early risers, and did they wake up cheerful and optimistic?

What time do you usually get out of bed in the morning?

Do you know some people who are obnoxiously cheerful in the morning?

What do you consider the benefits of being a night person?

Do you believe that being a morning person is a choice, or is it biological?

Alarm clock or wake up on your own?

What would you do with a couple of extra hours in the morning?

MOVIES

"Every great film should seem new every time you see it."

—Roger Ebert

"The older I get, the more I look at movies as a moving miracle. Audiences are harder to please if you're just giving them special effects...but they're easy to please if it's a good story."

—Steven Spielberg

Movies give you the power to experience life outside the boundaries of time and space. For two hours in the dark, you can travel to Mars, relive the Wild West, fall in love, and save the world from nuclear destruction.

———————————————————

What is your favorite movie?

Did your family like to watch movies together? Did you have movie night?

How many movies do you watch a month?

Do you have a favorite film genre? Director? Actor?

Is there one film that you can watch over and over again?

What is one film you know you're supposed to like but don't?

Do you like to watch movies at home or at the theater?

What is a film that you recently have recommended to your friends and family?

MOVING DAY

"That was the trouble with moving houses; no matter how carefully you packed the books, they never ended up on the new shelves in quite the right place."
—Val McDermid

"Home is a place you grow up wanting to leave, and grow old wanting to get back to."
—John Ed Pearce

Moving day can be exciting, but most people dread the thought. The furniture, the boxes, and the big screen TV test your physical strength, your friendships, and your ability to remember where you put the can opener.

How many times have you moved in your life?

Did you grow up in just one house or many?

Is there anything about moving into a new house or apartment that you really enjoy?

Do you move yourself or hire a moving company?

What dorm, house, or apartment was your favorite place?

Are you someone who will move many times, or do you like to stay in one place?

Is there one place you would like to live because of the weather, the culture, or the food?

What's one piece of advice you would give to someone who is packing up everything and moving to a new place?

MUSIC

"Where words leave off, music begins."
—Heinrich Heine

"Music is the divine way to tell beautiful, poetic things to the heart."
—Pablo Casals

Music is a gift from God. It is the perfect gift because it brings joy and pleasure to the composer, to the performer, to the listener, and especially to the one the music was written for. Music is a taste of heaven.

How important is music in your life?

Was there someone in your childhood who gave you an appreciation or interest in music?

How would you describe your taste in music?

Do you have a large music collection? How many songs do you own?

Does your music collection include vinyl? CDs? Cassette tapes? 8-track tapes?

What is your favorite piece of music or songwriter?

Have you ever studied music in a formal setting?

What do you think it means that music is a "universal language"?

MY BODY

"I don't want to wait until I'm 73 to embrace my body. To look back and think of my beauty: How did I miss it? Let's not wait another moment."

—Ashley Asti

"And I said to my body, softly, 'I want to be your friend.' It took a long breath, and replied, 'I have been waiting my whole life for this.'"

—Nayyirah Waheed

How wonderful it would be if we could love our bodies unconditionally. We would take better care of the inside and never waste a minute wishing we had flawless skin, a smaller nose, or a perfect figure.

What do you like about your body?

What is one thing you would change about your body if you could?

Do you believe you are taking good care of your body?

What is one thing you can control that would improve how you feel about your body?

Do you believe that plastic surgery and other procedures are perfectly acceptable ways to improve how you look?

Why is our society so obsessed with youth and beauty?

Is there someone you know who has taken care of their body and is aging gracefully?

How can you be more content with the body you've been given?

MY ROOM

"The cleanliness of my room reflects the stability of my life at any given point."

—Unknown

"My room is the only place in the world where I feel free, free to be myself."

—Ankur Mishra

There is a time early in life when you realize the importance of having your own space. If parents are wise, they allow their children to create a space that is an expression of who they are and all they want to be.

_____

How would you describe your room when you were a child?

Did you have to share a room with your siblings, or did you have a room all to yourself?

What is the first thing you ever remember putting up on the wall of your room?

Did you parents allow you to lock your bedroom door?

Were you a neat freak, or was your room a big, smelly mess?

What do you think are the benefits of allowing a child to arrange and decorate their bedroom any way they wish?

Is your childhood bedroom still accessible? Do your parents still live in the same house?

What do you think makes a space comfortable, safe, live-able, and an expression of you?

MY WEDDING DAY

"I don't want a fashionable wedding, but only those about me whom I love, and to them I wish to look and be my familiar self."

—Louisa May Alcott

"A wedding doesn't have to be expensive to be memorable."

—Colin Cowie

Few days receive more attention than your wedding day. Be sure the day is more about making meaning than making a statement. Statements are short-lived, but meaning lasts forever.

When was the first time you stopped to consider what your wedding day would be like?

Are you someone who enjoys all the details of planning a wedding, or is it something that gives you a headache?

What are some things you've seen other people do at their weddings that you would like to have in your own?

How much money is a reasonable amount to spend on a wedding?

Why is it important to get married in the presence of your friends and family?

Would you like to write your own vows to one another?

How do you think couples could spend time preparing for marriage as intensely as they prepare for the wedding?

MYSTERY

"The mystery of life isn't a problem to solve but a reality to experience."

—Frank Herbert

"Mysteries abound where most we seek for answers."

—Ray Bradbury

Mystery is often confused with ambiguity. Ambiguity assumes there is no proper interpretation and leaves the truth to the beholder, but mystery contends that the truth is out there and it's our job to find it.

Do you enjoy a good mystery?

How comfortable are you with the things in life that can't be explained?

How would you describe the difference between ambiguity and mystery?

Are you intrigued by the mysteries of the supernatural and life after death?

Why do you think the mystery genre is so popular?

Is there one aspect of life that is nothing more than one big mystery to you?

Have you ever sought to be a mystery to someone?

What would be some of the benefits of accepting the unexplainable mysteries of life?

MYTH

"I believe that legends and myths are largely made of truth."

—J.R.R. Tolkien

"A myth is a lie that conveys a truth."

—C.S. Lewis

A myth is a chalice so beautiful that the wine it holds is often overlooked. The value of a myth is not whether dragons exist but whether there are still brave souls to fight them.

Do you see value in studying Greek and Roman mythology?

What's your favorite myth?

Do you believe there are modern-day myths?

Are there legends and myths in your family that have been carried on for generations?

How can a myth that is factually untrue convey a far greater truth?

Do you value the truth of non-fiction over the truth of fiction?

Is there a myth-based film or novel that has been especially meaningful to you?

How can we preserve the value of storytelling, of sitting around the fire and telling the stories of who we are?

AUGUST 13

NAILS ON A CHALKBOARD

"In our society, the sound of men complaining is like nails on a chalkboard."
—Warren Farrell

Misophonist: Someone who has an extreme intolerance for certain sounds like gum smacking and nails on a chalkboard.

It may not be nails on a chalkboard, but there's something out there that drives you crazy. It may be incompetence or reckless driving, or someone who chews their ice, but all you can think is, "Stop it!"

Is there something that people do that drives you mad?

Are there any sounds, textures, or smells that make you sick?

Is there something you do that can make a friend's skin crawl?

Have you ever tried to ignore that thing that drives you crazy?

What's the oddest source of irritation you've ever observed?

Do you believe ancient cultures had the same annoying practices, or are we just getting soft?

Have you intentionally sought to annoy someone by doing that thing that drives them crazy?

NARCISSISM

"I don't care what you think unless it is about me."

—Kurt Cobain

"Narcissist: (n): a more polite term for a self-serving, manipulative, evil jerk with no soul and no compassion."

—Unknown

Most narcissists are convinced they are guilty of nothing more than a positive self-image, but their constant self-obsession leaves the rest of the world positively tired of hearing how "wonderful" they are.

———————————————

Do you have any narcissistic tendencies?

Would it be easier to start as a narcissist and pursue humility or have an inferiority complex and pursue healthy self-worth?

Is it possible for you to have as much compassion for someone who thinks highly of themselves as someone who doesn't?

Would you place yourself on the negative or positive side of a balanced and healthy understanding of yourself?

Who is someone who models for you a good and healthy expression of who they are?

Is there a book, course, or video that has helped you in pursuing a proper understanding of your self-worth?

What's one thing you can do this year to grow in developing a healthy self-perception?

NATIONALITY

"National pride is to countries what self-respect is to individuals: a necessary condition for self-improvement."

—Richard Rorty

"A wise nation preserves its records, gathers up its muniments, decorates the tombes of its illustrious dead, repairs its greatest structure and fosters national pride and love of country, by perpetual references to the sacrifices and glories of the past."

—Joseph Howe

Nationality is different from ethnicity. Nationality has nothing to do with what country your ancestors came from. Nationality is the status of belonging to a particular nation and choosing to defend it.

Do you take pride in your nationality?

How did you parents teach you to value your citizenship?

How will would you say you understand the history of the nation where you hold your citizenship?

Do you know anyone who has dual citizenship?

Do you have a passport, and have you traveled to another country where you were treated as a foreigner?

Have you ever considered changing your nationality?

What do you think about countries that require their citizens to serve in the military?

Do you feel most people take their nationality for granted?

NAUSEA

"No one dies of nausea, but it can seriously sap the will to live."
—Yann Martel

"The act of vomiting deserves your respect. It's an orchestral event of the gut."
—Mary Roach

Most of us have experienced the displeasure of nausea. When it reaches its natural conclusion it, produces a gut-wrenching eruption that can only be described as a private matter that doesn't appreciate an audience.

When was the last time you threw up?

Are there smells or sights that cause you to experience nausea?

Do you say, "I'm nauseous" or "I'm nauseated?"

Do you have an embarrassing "throw up" story?

When you're nauseated, do you camp out in the bathroom or walk around with a bucket?

Do you have any special remedies for nausea?

Have you ever been so sick that you lost fluids to the point of being hospitalized?

What's the best way to help someone who is sick with nausea and vomiting?

NEIGHBORHOODS

"You can take the guy out of the neighborhood, but you can't take the neighborhood out of the guy."
—Frankie Valli

"It is discouraging to try to be a good neighbor in a bad neighborhood."
—William Castle

Neighborhoods are the fabric of America. It's the closest thing we have to villages, where families look out for each other, children play together, and everyone knows everyone's secrets.

———————————————

Do you have an attachment to the neighborhood where you grew up?

How did you parents choose the house where you grew up, and how did they interact with your neighbors?

Is the neighborhood where you grew up the same today as it was when you were a child?

Did your childhood neighborhood have a specific ethnic flavor, or was it a diverse mix of cultures?

Who were some of the kids from the neighborhood that you played with?

Do you want to live in a similar neighborhood to the one you grew up in?

What do we lose when we no longer have neighborhoods that are close-knit and supportive?

NIGHTMARES

"Of all the things you choose in life, you don't get to choose what your nightmares are. You don't pick them; they pick you."

—John Irving

"They've promised that dreams can come true, but forgot to mention that nightmares are dreams, too."

—Oscar Wilde

Researchers say that nightmares are the brain's way of focusing our attention on things we need to address. If that's the case, many of us need to pack an extra set of clothes and a parachute.

Do you have reoccurring nightmares?

Can you trace the reason for your nightmares?

Do your dreams and nightmares seem to be random, or are you able to interpret what's going on in your head?

Do you believe that what you eat affects your dreams?

Why do you think so many people have bad dreams about giving a speech where they're unprepared and not properly dressed?

Do you have really scary nightmares with monsters, violence, and horrific events?

Can you control your dreams?

What is one thing you believe your brain is trying to purge through the dreams and nightmares you experience?

AUGUST 19

NOISE

"Of all the varieties of modern pollution, noise is the most insidious."

—Robert Lacey

"Noise pollution is a relative thing. In a city, it's a jet plane taking off. In a monastery, it's a pen that scratches."

—Robert Orben

Noise is the word we use to describe sound in its negative form. *Noise* can also be used to describe any form of distraction or clutter. We shouldn't learn to live with the *noise* we should learn to remove it.

How do you cope with the "noise" in your life?

How can the word *noise* be used to describe sources of irritation and distraction beyond sound?

How do you block out distracting, physical noise when you're trying to concentrate?

How do you block out the metaphorical noise in your life?

Would you characterize the place where you live to be noisy or quiet?

Do you believe noise is something you could get used to, like living on a flight path or next to the subway?

Would you say your household growing up was especially loud and noisy?

Do you believe we need laws that protect communities from excessive noise?

OPPRESSION

"The most potent weapon of the oppressor is the mind of the oppressed."

—Steven Biko

"If you are neutral on situations of injustice, you have chosen the side of the oppressor."

—Desmond Tutu

Oppression is the misuse of power and authority, and it is often expressed in subtle and imperceptible ways. Influential people would be wise to contemplate how their power affects others.

———————————————————

Do you see subtle or overt forms of oppression in the world around you?

Have you ever experienced oppression because of your race, ethnicity, social status, or other issue?

Are you currently in a role of authority where you might need to contemplate how your power affects the people under you?

What is your awareness of the realities of extreme oppression in the world today?

Have you ever considered getting personally involved in the fight against oppression?

Do you believe that some people are allowing themselves to be oppressed when they could easily escape it?

What are some things you might do this year to increase your knowledge and awareness of oppression in the world?

OPTIMISM

"I say looking on the bright side of life never killed anybody."

—Jenny Han

"Optimism doesn't wait on facts. It deals with prospects."

—Norman Cousins

To be an optimist is a choice, and it's a good one. Some say being optimistic has a positive effect on achieving success, but regardless of the outcome, being optimistic is what brings joy to the journey.

Would you consider yourself to be an optimist?

How did your parents view life—were they optimists or pessimists?

Is there any validity to the notion that believing good things will happen causes good things to happen?

How does someone's attitude toward life affect whether you want to be around them?

Is there someone in your life whose positive outlook and optimism are contagious?

Do you currently have an optimistic attitude about a future outcome?

Do you think the power of positive thinking is false?

How can someone change from being a negative person to being a positive person?

ORGANIZED

"For every minute spent in organizing, an hour is earned."

—Benjamin Franklin

*"You may say organize, organize, organize; but there may
be so much organization that it will interfere with the work
to be done."*

—Mark Twain

**Being organized is not the same as being effective.
Some very effective and highly successful people are
completely unorganized, but for most of us, being more
organized would help our chances.**

Would you consider yourself to be an organized person?

How did your parents model good organizational skills?

Is there one area of your life that is in critical need of being organized?

Do you believe that it's possible to make organization your main focus and, as a result, productivity suffers?

Have you ever read a book or watched a tutorial on how to be more organized?

What systems, folders, or apps do you use to be more organized?

Are you content with the level of organization in your life, or do you want to improve?

PAIN

"If you love deeply, you're going to get hurt badly. But it's still worth it."

—C.S. Lewis

"Given the choice between the experience of pain and nothing, I would choose pain."

—William Faulkner

A life without pain would only reduce our understanding of pleasure. We enjoy food because of hunger and rest because of fatigue. The pain we experience in life opens the possibility for great pleasure.

———————————————————

What is the most physically painful thing you've ever experienced?

How would you compare physical pain to emotional pain?

How have you experienced emotional pain in your life?

Are you currently living with some form of chronic pain?

What is your remedy for physical pain?

What is your remedy for emotional pain?

How has the pain in your life caused you to grow and mature?

What do you think Nietzsche meant when he said, "That which does not kill us makes us stronger"?

PARTIES

"No one looks back on their life and remembers the nights they got plenty of sleep."

—Unknown

"Life may not be the party we hoped for, but while we're here we should dance."

—Unknown

Party, *fiesta*, *soirée*, there's a word for celebrations in every language. The human race has learned not only to survive but to thrive. Sadly, in our thriving we have reduced our parties to cake, candles, and a few games.

Do you like parties?

What were parties like in your house when you were a child?

When was the last time you attended a party?

Do you dance at parties? Drink? Overeat?

What's the most lavish, expensive party you've ever been to?

What would you consider to be a valid reason to throw a party?

Do you believe our culture has reduced parties to social obligations instead of celebratory feasts?

Who is someone in your life that would benefit from a party thrown in their honor?

How can you develop a greater spirit of celebration in your life?

PATIENCE

"Patience is bitter, but its fruit is sweet."
—Jean-Jacques Rousseau

"Patience is not simply the ability to wait; it's how we behave while we're waiting."
—Joyce Meyer

Patience is a virtue not of endurance but of faith. Patience believes that what we are waiting for will come to pass and that it will be worth the wait.

Are you a patient person?

How did your parents model patience for you as a child?

In what area of your life are you least likely to demonstrate patience?

What are some experiences and circumstances that have developed patience in your life?

Was there ever a time when you thought your patience demonstrated nothing more than passivity when you should have demanded satisfaction?

Who is someone who has been extremely patient with you?

Is there someone who would benefit from your patience?

What advice would you give to someone who wanted to develop patience?

How would you like to visibly demonstrate greater patience this year?

PEACE

"Lord, make me an instrument of your peace. Where there is hatred, let me sow love."

—Francis of Assisi

"Mankind must remember that peace is not God's gift to his creatures; peace is our gift to each other."

—Elie Wiesel

Peace is the absence of conflict. It is the wonderful state of feeling safe and serene. Perfect peace is feeling safe and serene even though we're surrounded by conflict.

Would you consider yourself to be at peace?

How do you seek to protect and provide peace in your life?

What produces the greatest stress and conflict in your life and robs you of peace?

Have you ever lived in a country at war?

Do you believe that the military might produce peace through intimidation?

Is there one historical figure you admire for their role in bringing peace?

What do you consider to be one of the most peaceful countries in the world?

How can governments do a better job to pursue peace?

What's one thing you could do this year to bring more peace into your life?

PERFECTIONISM

"Perfectionism is the voice of the oppressor."
—Anne Lamott

"Many people think of perfectionism as striving to be your best, but it is not about self-improvement; it's about earning approval and acceptance."
—Brené Brown

To be perfect is impossible, but that never seems to stop us. The reality of perfection is like a star in the night sky: We see it clearly, we know it exists, and we can't help but dream of ways to get up there.

Would you consider yourself a perfectionist?

How have you observed perfectionism expressed in your family and friends?

Has the desire to be perfect at something kept you from moving forward?

Would you rather be a perfectionist than someone who lacks excellence?

Is there some field or craft where perfection can actually be measured objectively and therefore achieved?

What is one thing you would like to do perfectly?

How do you teach someone to be content with being less than perfect?

How can you extend grace to yourself in areas where you are less than perfect?

PERFORMING

"If you have stage fright, it never goes away. But then I wonder: Is the key to that magical performance because of fear?"
—Stevie Nicks

"All the world's a stage, and most of us are desperately unrehearsed."
—Sean O'Casey

A performance represents a challenge for you to get out of the way. It's the performer's job to take the music or the script and express it so the audience can experience all the author intended.

Do you see yourself as a performer?

When was the first time you had to present something to an audience?

How have you found ways to cope with stage fright or performance jitters?

Do you have a favorite performer that makes their craft seem effortless?

Have you ever had the dream of being a famous actor, singer, or public speaker?

What was the largest audience you've ever had to address?

What is the most money you've ever spent for a ticket for a live performance?

What is one way you can develop your performance skills?

PERSEVERANCE

"Perseverance is not a long race; it is many short races one after the other."

—Walter Elliot

"Perseverance is stubbornness with a purpose."

—Josh Shipp

To persevere is to pursue a goal despite all difficulties, obstacles, and discouragement. Perseverance assumes the presence of adversity but chooses to respond with greater determination.

In what ways have you had to demonstrate perseverance in your life?

Have you ever participated in an extreme challenge that has forced you to physically persevere?

Have you ever given up when you know you should have kept going?

Do you have a role model or person who inspires you to keep going when you feel like giving up?

What is the most difficult thing you've ever attempted to achieve?

What is one thing you would do if you knew you couldn't fail?

How do you think people develop the mental toughness to never give up?

Is there something you need to do this year that is hard?

PERSONAL BEST

"Your personal best is the best in the world."
—Ashton Eaton

"Success is a personal matter; only you as an individual can tell if you did everything within your power to give your best effort."
—John Wooden

One of the best days of your life is the day you stop competing with others and start competing with yourself. There is great value in learning to give your very best and then pushing yourself to do better.

Are you a competitive person?

What is your first memory of being placed into a competitive situation?

Do you struggle with comparison and competing against others instead of with yourself?

Do you have any personal goals that you are trying to exceed?

What is one thing that you would like to do better?

Have you ever followed a routine or regiment designed to help you improve at a sport, craft, or skill?

Is there a race, tournament, or competition you should enter this year to push yourself?

How can you convert traditional forms of competition into personal challenges?

PERSONAL HYGIENE

"Indeed, personal hygiene heals more than doctor's prescribed medicines."

—Andoh Francis

"If you don't smell good, then you don't look good."

—Katy Elizabeth

Personal hygiene is a form of self-respect. When you care for yourself in this way, you present yourself as a person of great worth, and others will see you that way too.

How would you rate yourself in the area of personal hygiene?

How did your parents teach you about the importance of showers, shampoo, toothpaste, and deodorant?

What are your favorite personal hygiene products?

Do you shower or bathe every day?

When was the last time you went to the dentist?

Have you ever had to tell someone they had B.O. or bad breath?

Is it possible to go to extremes when it comes to personal hygiene?

What is one area of personal hygiene that could use some improvement in your life?

Have you ever judged someone because of a hygiene issue?

WORK

"Opportunity is missed by most people because it is dressed in overalls and looks like work."
—Thomas Edison

"When your work speaks for itself, don't interrupt."
—Henry J. Kaiser

Labor Day is the day we pay tribute to the value of hard work. Some people see work as a necessary evil, but if you love what you do, work is an expression of who you are, and how you make your contribution to the world.

Do you like to work?

How did your family think and talk about work? Was it an opportunity or a drudgery?

Is there someone in your life that showed you the value of hard work?

What kind of work makes life miserable for you?

Are there some things you do for work that don't feel like work?

Do you enjoy tough, physical labor that makes you sweat and pushes your body?

Do you think you would be happy if you never had to work another day in your life?

How does your job fit your natural strengths and abilities?

What is one thing you can do to make work a more positive experience?

PERSONAL RETREATS

"Within you there is a stillness and sanctuary to which you can retreat at any time and be yourself."
—Hermann Hesse

"Sometimes I need to go off on my own. I'm not sad. I'm not angry. I'm recharging my batteries."
—Kristen Butler

Take time, at least once a year, to escape your routine, turn off your phone, and just reflect. It can be a weekend, an overnight, or just a few hours, but your mind and soul need time to recalibrate.

Have you ever had the chance to take a retreat?

How could a personal retreat help when things in your life seem to be spinning out of control?

Have you ever practiced quiet contemplation or meditation?

How does it make you feel to spend long periods of time alone?

Have you ever experienced a time when you needed to get away and figure things out?

If you were to spend a weekend alone to think and reflect, where would you go?

What's the longest time you've been disconnected from your phone, email, social media, and the Internet?

How would your life improve from spending time alone?

PERSONALITY PROFILES

"The shoe that fits one person pinches another; there is no recipe for living that suits all cases."
—Carl Jung

"The Enneagram doesn't put you in a box; it helps you get out of the box you're already in."
—Callie Ammons

Aristotle categorizes people based on four body fluids, Myers-Briggs uses 16 personality types, and the Enneagram divides the world into nine. Perhaps these tools over-simplify things, but it's a useful place to start.

Have you ever taken a personality profile test?

Have you been exposed to different types of personality profile tools and resources?

Do you have a preferred profile that you like to use?

Have you found these resources to be helpful in understanding your family, friends, and co-workers?

What would be the downside to putting too much stock into this way of understanding people?

Can you think of one relationship that has benefited from using a personality profile?

Do you feel like you have a better understanding of yourself based on these tools?

Who is someone you would like to get to know better?

PESSIMISM

"My pessimism extends to the point of even suspecting the sincerity of other pessimists."

—Jean Rostand

"I'd rather be optimistic and wrong than pessimistic and right."

—Elon Musk

Pessimism is the perfect remedy for avoiding disappointment. A pessimist has no hopes to dash or dreams to shatter. They always expect the worst, so anything better than that is a bonus.

What are some positive things that come out of pessimism?

How would you explain the difference between pessimism and realism?

How have you seen pessimism expressed in your life?

Have you ever had to end a friendship or cut off a relationship because that person was so negative?

Do you believe that being a pessimist is genetic and just a part of who a person might be, or is it a choice?

How do you like to receive negative news about a future prospect?

How can you learn to respond to negativity in positive and healthy ways?

PET PEEVES

"I don't have pet peeves; I have whole kennels of irritation."

—Whoopi Goldberg

"Everything that irritates us about others can lead us to an understanding of ourselves."

—Carl Jung

You know it shouldn't bother you as much as it does, but you can't help it. It's that minor annoyance that drives you crazy. Keep it a secret, or someone will be sure to torture you with it for the rest of your life.

Do you have a pet peeve?

What do you think are some of the most common pet peeves?

Are you aware of the pet peeves of your friends and family members?

Have you ever purposely tried to annoy someone because you knew their pet peeves?

Is it possible to overcome a pet peeve, or should we embrace them as a quirky part of who we are?

What's the strangest pet peeve you've ever heard of?

Have you acquired any new pet peeves in the last year or recent past?

How can you turn your pet peeves from negatives to positives?

PETS

"You can usually tell that a man is good if he has a dog who loves him."

—W. Bruce Cameron

"There is no psychiatrist in the world like a puppy licking your face."

—Bernard Williams

A pet is a domesticated animal that brings joy and affection. The word *pet* comes from Scotland, when, one day, back in the 1500s, a farmer looked around at all the animals on the farm and picked his favorite.

Do you have a pet?

What did your parents think about having pets? Did you grow up with dogs, cats, goldfish, or other pets?

What are the names of your pets past and present?

Do you know someone who seems to love their pet a little too much?

Is there anything wrong with substituting a relationship with people for a relationship with your pet?

Is it odd that people are willing to go out in the freezing cold and follow their dogs around with little poop bags?

If you could have any pet in the world, what animal would you choose?

How could caring for an animal make you a better person?

PHILANTHROPY

"If you're the luckiest 1% of humanity, you owe it to the rest of humanity to think about the other 99%."
—Warren Buffet

"Philanthropy is not about money...it's about feeling the pain of others and caring enough about their needs to help."
—Timothy Pina

Philanthropy literally means "love of mankind." In its practical expression, it describes generous acts, usually donating money, to benefit a purpose or cause. It is a beautiful thing, especially when done anonymously.

Do you make contributions to help a cause?

Are there certain charities or non-profit organizations that you think are doing a good job?

Have you had the opportunity to see firsthand how a charitable organization has made a practical difference?

Do you research organizations before you donate?

Have you ever considered working full-time for a non-profit organization?

Do you ever feel guilt for not giving more or doing more for those who are in need?

What are the needs in this world that most concern you?

How can you grow in compassion for those less fortunate than you?

GRANDMOTHERS

"Truth be told, being a grandma is as close as we ever get to perfection."

—Bryna Nelson Paston

"If nothing is going well, call your grandmother."

—Italian Proverb

Grandmothers are perfect for grandchildren. They have lots of love and lots of time, without the parental responsibility to correct or discipline. It frees them up to break a few rules and spoil their grandchildren.

Do you have a close relationship with your grandmother?

What is the first memory you have of your grandmother?

Did your grandparents live close to you when you were a child, or did you have to travel to see them?

What are some favorite memories you have of your grandmother?

Was your grandmother the kind that liked to spoil you with candy, presents, and toys?

How would you describe your grandmother?

When was the last time you saw your grandmother, and what did you do together?

What do you think makes a really great grandmother?

PHOBIAS

"Fear is the path to the dark side. Fear leads to anger, anger leads to hate, hate leads to suffering."
—Yoda (Star Wars)

"Do the thing you fear to do and keep on doing it...that is the quickest and surest way ever yet discovered to conquer fear."
—Dale Carnegie

Phobia is the clinical word for fear. Fears come in all shapes and sizes, and some can be quite quirky and irrational. Clowns may not be scary to you, but not everyone is in a hurry to buy a ticket for the circus.

———————————————

What are you afraid of?

What were the things you were afraid of as a child?

Do you think there is a difference between a fear and a phobia?

Is all fear bad, or can it be healthy?

How do you cope with fear?

Are you living in fear of something?

What's the most irrational fear you've ever experienced?

Have you ever had to hold someone's hand or talk them off the ledge when they were crippled with fear?

How can you remove the fear in your life and grow to live without the anxiety it produces?

PHONES

"The cell phone has become the adult's transitional object, replacing the toddler's teddy bear for comfort and a sense of belonging."
—Margaret Hefferman

"The average smartphone user checks his or her device every six and a half minutes."
—Arianna Huffington

How would Alexander Graham Bell react to what his invention has become? He would be shocked to find that his invention has become more than just a phone; it's a camera, a computer, an extension of our brain.

———————————————————

How would you describe your relationship with your phone?

Do you think it's odd that we would even use the word *relationship* to describe how we interact with technology?

How much time do you think you spend each day using your phone?

Have you ever decided to stop using your phone for an extended period of time?

Are you concerned with what the smartphone has become in today's society?

What phone do you own, and are you happy with it?

What are some steps you can take to keep the phone in its proper place?

9/11

"On September 11, I always take the day off. I want to be in a peaceful, quiet place praying. It is a day I both mourn and celebrate."

—Genelle Guzman-McMillan, 9/11 Survivor

"September 11, 2001, revealed heroism in ordinary people who might have gone through their lives never called upon to demonstrate the extent of their courage."

—Geraldine Brooks

There are moments that make history, and the morning of September 11, 2001, is one of them. People used to ask, "What were you doing when Kennedy was shot?" Now they ask, "Where were you on 9/11?"

What were you doing on September 11, 2001?

Do you know anyone who was personally impacted by the attacks of that day?

Have you ever been to New York city and visited Ground Zero?

Did life in the USA change forever because of that day?

Why did so many people go to church the Sunday after 9/11?

Are statues and monuments a good way to keep memories alive?

Do you believe that the war on terrorism is a winnable war?

How important is it to remember the events of 9/11?

PIZZA

"Unless you are a pizza, the answer is yes, I can live without you."

—Bill Murray

"Pizza is a circle. Pizza is my life. Pizza is the circle of life."

—Ed Sheeran

Pizza is the perfect food. It's inexpensive, customizable, easy to eat, and fun to share. If you want an interesting conversation, ask someone who makes the best pizza.

———————————

How important is pizza?

Who makes the best pizza?

What do you like on your pizza?   Are you into pineapple and anchovies?

Chicago or New York style?

Is there one topping that makes a pizza inedible for you?

What is the most pizza you've ever eaten in one sitting?

Was there a pizza joint in your neighborhood?

Do you dine in, pick up, or have your pizza delivered?

Have you ever tried to make your own pizza?

How often do you have pizza?

PLACES YOU'VE BEEN

"A person susceptible to 'wanderlust' is not so much addicted to movement as committed to transformation."

—Pico Iyer

"Once the travel bug bites there is no known antidote, and I know that I shall be happily infected until the end of my life."

—Michael Palin

People keep track of all the places they've visited. A "place" can be so many things: a country, a state, a park, or a restaurant. People will walk across a border for 10 seconds, just long enough so they can tell the story.

Do you like to travel?

What is the most interesting place you've ever been?

Do you have a list of places you would like to visit?

Do you have a goal to visit all the states in the USA, or all the national parks, or all the shoe stores in New York city?

Have you had the opportunity to travel internationally?

Do you have a passport? How many countries have you visited?

Do you have a travel budget for trips and vacations?

Do you have a "trip from hell" story?

Do you have a favorite mode of travel—car, train, ship, or airplane?

What is the value of experiencing new places in the world?

PLAY

"Play is our brain's favorite way of learning."

—Diane Ackerman

"We don't stop playing because we grow old; we grow old because we stop playing."

—George Bernard Shaw

Play is not the stuff of children but the sign of a healthy mind. It's permission to imagine and pretend, to work without expectation, and to enjoy the process. And to think, for some people, that describes their job.

———————————————

Is play still a part of your life?

How would you define what it means to play?

Was your childhood filled with a sufficient amount of play?

How did you play as a child? Did you play make-believe?

What are some of your favorite memories of playing with your siblings or friends?

Do you have a need for more play in your life?

What are some activities you enjoy doing for leisure, fun, and exercise?

Is there something that was once play but now seems childish?

How can you intentionally bring more playtime into your life?

POETRY

"Poetry is language at its most distilled and most powerful."

—Rita Dove

"Poetry is when an emotion has found its thought and the thought has found words."

—Robert Frost

Roses are red, and violets are blue; we often fear poetry because of the rules. Poetry is the art of setting words to rhythm and rhyme. It's an amazing way to express your feelings and ideas. Don't let the rules stop you!

Do you like poetry?

Have you ever studied poetry or taken a creative writing class on poetry?

Do you have a favorite poem, poet, or collection of poems?

Have you ever written a poem?

Have you ever written a poem as an expression of your love for someone?

Can you name any famous poets?

Do you feel that poetry is just for those who are overly emotional and romantic?

What's one reason you could think of to write a poem this week?

How might you increase your appreciation for poetry?

POLITICS

"Politics is the art of looking for trouble, finding it everywhere, diagnosing it incorrectly, and applying the wrong remedies."

—Ernest Benn

"Politics is war without bloodshed, while war is politics with bloodshed."

—Mao Zedong

It could be argued that politics, like journalism, have lost their way. Politics and politicians seem to be more interested in wielding power and promoting partisan issues than making life better for the people they serve.

Do you like to discuss politics?

How did your parents express their political views?

Do you have strong political views? Are you committed to a particular political party or agenda?

How can the profession of serving as a politician be redeemed, reinvented, or improved?

Would you ever consider running for public office?

Are there some politicians who have earned your trust and who you believe are making a positive difference?

Is your political party the political party of your family, friends, city, or region?

How can people with different views begin to have healthy dialogue and discussion about politics?

POVERTY

"The real tragedy of the poor is the poverty of their aspirations."

—Adam Smith

"Poverty is the worst form of violence."

—Mahatma Gandhi

Poverty is far more than the absence of wealth. True poverty is a defeated soul with no hope or dream. Without hope, life ceases to have meaning. And meaning is what makes life humane.

Have you ever been poor?

How would you describe the financial situation of your family as a child?

Do you believe there is a difference between the absence of wealth and poverty?

Have you ever found yourself in a place without hope?

Do you believe you have a proper perspective of money, wealth, and prosperity?

How would you describe your level of concern and compassion for the poor?

Is there some area of your life that is spiritually and emotionally impoverished?

How can you be more proactive in eliminating poverty?

PRAGMATISM

"Pragmatism is nothing without imagination; and imagination is wasted without pragmatism."

—Robert Holstock

"Pursue your passion, and everything else will fall into place. This not being romantic. This is the highest order of pragmatism."

—Gabby Giffords

Pragmatism believes that expending energy and effort is only justified if success is guaranteed. Pragmatism makes a lot of sense when you can't risk losing your job or leave the rent to chance.

Would you consider yourself a pragmatist?

Where would your parents fall on the scale between risk-taking and pragmatism?

In what areas of your life would you consider yourself to be conservative, careful, and pragmatic?

Would you benefit from becoming more of a risk-taker or becoming more cautious and pragmatic?

Would you consider fear to be the number one motivation for pragmatism?

What is one thing you could do that would represent taking a risk?

Is there someone in your life who frustrates you with their pragmatic behavior?

PRETENDING

"Be careful what you pretend to be because you are what you pretend to be."
—Kurt Vonnegut

"Pretending is a very valuable life skill."
—Meryl Streep

Pretending is often considered to be childish behavior. As an adult, it carries the shame of posing, faking, and lying. There needs to be a grown-up word for pretending, one that allows our imagination to keep growing.

Did you like to pretend as a child?

Who did you pretend to be, and what did you pretend to do?

Was there a time when you felt pretending was a childish thing that needed to stop?

What do you think about cosplay, costume parties, and other forms of grown-up pretending?

Would you consider films, plays, and theatrical performances as an opportunity to pretend?

Do you have a good imagination, and are you still using it today?

How can the magic and wonder of pretending be kept alive throughout our lives?

PRIDE

"Pride is spiritual cancer: it eats up the very possibility of love, contentment, or even common sense."
—C.S. Lewis

"Pride is nothing more than false courage without long-term solutions."
—Shannon L. Alder

Pride can be a great quality or the worst quality ever. They say pride is the root of all evil, but they also say to take pride in your work, your family, your school, and your country.

———————————————

How is pride expressed both positively and negatively in your life?

How would you explain the difference between bad pride and good pride?

Have you ever been humbled by the circumstances of life?

How does the pride you have in your work and accomplishments produce better results?

Do you believe that your mom and dad are proud of you?

Why does it matter so much what our parents think of us?

Do you need to let someone know that you are proud of them?

How can we humble ourselves and remove negative pride?

PRINCE CHARMING

"I don't need the prince charming to have my own happy ending."

—Katy Perry

"He's not your prince charming if he doesn't make sure you know that you're his princess."

—Demi Lovato

The notion of "prince charming" represents all the truth and tragedy of fairy tales. The truth reveals an ideal that men should aspire to be. The tragedy is a woman who fixates on the fantasy instead of accepting an imperfect man who truly loves her.

Do you value the message of fairy tales?

What are some of your favorite fairy tales and fables from childhood?

Do you believe the fantasy of a prince charming or perfect princess has a negative effect on our expectations?

What do you see as the qualities and characteristics a prince charming character represents?

Is there one fairy tale that does a better job of representing what a prince charming truly should be?

Do you have a list of qualities that you are looking for in a life partner?

How can you work on being a better person instead of looking for the perfect one?

PROCRASTINATION

"Procrastination is like a credit card: it's a lot of fun until you get the bill."
—Christopher Parker

"Procrastination is opportunity's assassin."
—Victor Kiam

Procrastination is a by-product of laziness and fear. It's a coping mechanism that allows us to delay the pain of work and/or the fear of failure. Some people believe they only do their best work the hour before it's due.

Are you prone to procrastinate?

How do you work under the pressure of a deadline? Do you perform better or worse?

Have you learned to delay gratification and do the hard and difficult thing now?

What are some tasks or activities you tend to delay?

Is there a hard job or task you always do right away and without delay?

Have you ever been forced to stay up all night or work an entire weekend because of your procrastination?

What is the motive behind your tendency to procrastinate?

What are two or three things you would like to learn to do without procrastination?

PUBERTY

"What happens when children reach puberty earlier and adulthood later? The answer is a good deal of teenage weirdness."
—Alison Gopnik

"Other than dying, I think puberty is probably about as rough as it gets."
—Rick Springfield

Some adolescents seem to enter a cocoon on Friday and on Monday emerge as handsome men and beautiful women. For others, puberty is three years of biological warfare that can only be described as awkward.

Was puberty kind to you?

Did you have the "birds and the bees" conversation with your parents?

How did you respond to the physical changes in your body during puberty?

Did you go through puberty earlier or later than your peers?

How can parents, teachers, and the community help adolescents transition more easily through puberty?

What was the most awkward moment or issue for you during this time?

If you could go back in time, what would you say to yourself going through this awkward stage?

PUBLIC SPEAKING

"Public speaking professionals say that you win or lose the battle to hold your audience in the first 30 seconds of a given presentation."

—John Medina

"There are only two types of speakers in the world: the nervous and liars."

—Mark Twain

Delivering a good speech can be reduced to three things: Believe in what you have to say; believe it will help those who hear it; and believe it's your job to deliver it without getting in the way.

How comfortable do you feel giving a public speech?

Do you remember the first time you were required to give a speech in class?

Do you remember one or two speeches you gave at school?

When was the last time you gave a speech in public?

Is there some aspect of your job or personal life that requires you to speak in public on a regular basis?

Who do you think are some of the best presenters, preachers, or speakers?

Would you like to do more public speaking if given the opportunity?

What is one message you think is important to share with the world?

QUIET DESPERATION

"Most men lead lives of quiet desperation and go to the grave with the song still in them."

—Henry David Thoreau

"The soul yearns to escape the quiet desperation it lives in everyday… find the escape, heal the soul."

—Jamie Hannigan

Is compromise the curse of modern men and women? Perhaps the comforts and conventions of a mortgage, a car payment, and a credit card keep us from sailing the seven seas and pursuing other wild dreams.

Does Thoreau's line "Most men lead lives of quiet desperation" seem true?

What do you think he meant by that line?

Is there someone you know who is living the opposite of that depressing existence?

How do you believe the simplicity movement and the tiny house phenomenon opened doors for people to experience more from life?

Have you ever considered simplifying your life so you could be free to do more?

Is satisfaction with life just a myth?

How can you grow in your understanding of who you are and what your purpose in life might be?

QUIRKY HABITS

"Certain aspects of my personality are always going to come out on-screen. I guess that's just me—if they say I'm quirky, I'm quirky. It's better than being boring."

—Zooey Deschanel

"I'm not strange, weird, off, nor crazy, my reality is just different from yours."

—Lewis Carroll

Everyone should have a few quirky habits. They make you memorable, unique, and they make you, you. So go for it: knock three times, avoid cracks on the sidewalk, and wear your lucky socks. Put the YOU in unique!

———————————————————

Do you have any quirky habits?

How about your parents, grandparents, aunts, uncles, brothers, and sisters—do they do odd things?

What is the quirkiest thing you ever observed someone doing?

If you had to come up with a really quirky habit, what would it be?

Are there any quirky habits that you think actually might be quite helpful?

Is there a quirky habit you wish someone would stop doing?

Can you think of any common behavior in the world today that at one time had to be a very odd and quirky thing?

QUITTING

"If I quit now, I will be back to where I started, and when I started I was desperately wishing to be where I am now."

—Unknown

"Many of life's failures are people who did not realize how close they were to success when they gave up."

—Thomas Edison

The value of quitting is predicated on the thing you're choosing to quit. If it's smoking, then go all in. If it's quitting school, well that's usually unwise. The secret is knowing the difference between virtue and vice.

Are you someone who refuses to quit or give up?

What is something you quit but wish you continued?

What is something you quit and are glad you did?

Do you have any vices or bad habits that you know you need to quit?

Is there a good habit or discipline in your life that you want to stop or quit because it's too hard?

Have you ever quit your job?

What would you say to a young man or woman who wanted to drop out of school?

Who has been an inspiration in your life that motivates you to keep going?

Is there someone you could encourage to not give up?

READING

"Books are the plane and the train and the road. They are the destination and the journey. They are home."

—Anna Quindlen

"Reading gives us some place to go when we have to stay where we are."

—Mason Cooley

Reading increases your vocabulary and develops your communication skills. Reading is learning, traveling, and adventure without leaving home. Reading slows you down and grows your imagination. It's a great workout for the mind.

———————————————

Do you like to read?

Did you like to read as a child?

What were some of your favorite books when you were growing up?

Are you reading a book right now?

If you were to recommend a book to someone, what would you recommend?

Are you a fan of fiction or non-fiction?

Have you read the Harry Potter series, or some other series of books?

What is the greatest benefit that comes from reading?

RELAXATION

"Stop a minute, right where you are. Tell that imperious voice in your head to be still."

—Barbara Kingsolver

"Tension is who you think you should be. Relaxation is who you are."

—Chinese Proverb

We all have an idea of what it means to relax. Relaxation can be quiet and restful; it can also be loud and sweaty, like playing in a rock band. Relaxation might be best defined as something that doesn't take life but gives it.

How do you like to relax?

Do you build time for relaxation into your schedule?

What are some activities that give you life?

Do you believe it's important to spend money on relaxation, or is everything you need to relax completely free?

Is there a spa, a massage, or other activity that really relaxes you?

Are there some nervous, jittery people in your life in need of serious relaxation?

When you relax, are you usually looking to be alone or with other people?

How can you begin to develop a more intentional and regular practice of relaxation?

RELIGION

"Religion is the search for ultimate meaning."

—Viktor Frankl

"We have just enough religion to make us hate, but not enough to make us love one another."

—Jonathan Swift

It has been said that religion is man's feeble attempt to find God. It represents our insatiable need and desire to understand where we came from, why we're here, and where we're going.

———————————————

Would you consider yourself to be religious?

Did you grow up practicing a particular religion, and was your family devout?

How would you respond to someone who believes religions around the world have done more harm than good?

Have you ever considered leaving your religion or adopting a new one?

What do you believe are the strongest arguments for or against God?

Do you practice any spiritual disciplines, like meditation, attending church, celebrating holidays, fasting, or prayer?

Do you believe it's important for a married couple to share the same faith?

How can you develop your spiritual life?

RESPECT

"Respect yourself and others will respect you."

—Confucius

"I firmly believe that respect is a lot more important, and a lot greater, than popularity."

—Julius Irving

If you want to be respected, then you must live a life worthy of respect. Don't allow outside voices to determine your worth. The wise set their own bar and respect themselves based on always doing their best.

Do you have a healthy amount of self-respect?

What does it mean to respect someone?

Is it possible to respect someone's position but not respect who they are as a person?

Who are some people who have earned your greatest respect?

Is there one flaw, weakness, sin, or act that immediately causes you to lose respect for someone?

Do you respect your parents?

What's one quality, discipline, or achievement that would raise your level of respect for yourself or someone else?

Do you believe everyone deserves respect?

How could you increase the level of respect you have for yourself?

RETIREMENT

"My parents didn't want to move to Florida, but they turned sixty and that's the law."
—Jerry Seinfeld

"Often when you think you're at the end of something, you're at the beginning of something else."
—Fred Rogers

The idea of retirement is a relatively new idea in the history of mankind. Of course, life expectancy is a lot higher than it was in the 18th century. Now it's possible you could be relaxing by the pool for 40-50 years.

Are you currently planning and saving for retirement?

How have your grandparents or parents demonstrated the upside and downside of retirement?

At what age would you like to retire?

What would be the benefit of eliminating retirement as an option and pursuing meaningful work till you die?

Is there an activity or hobby you would like to pursue in retirement?

How will you know if you have enough money and savings to retire?

Do you have confidence that Social Security and other government programs will be there when you retire?

How can you begin to prepare for retirement now?

OCTOBER 03

REVERENCE

"Reverence for life is the highest court of appeal."

—Albert Schweitzer

"Reverence makes it possible to be whole, though ignorant. It is the wholeness of understanding."

—Wendell Berry

Reverence is a virtue on the verge of extinction. We have lost the value we once had for the sacred and holy. But those who still hold it high know the wonder and awe of being in the presence of the divine.

What does it mean to be reverent?

Do you revere something or someone?

What do you believe are the reasons modern society seems to have little interest in the sacred and holy?

Is it possible to have reverence without some level of humility and healthy fear?

Are the things that produce reverence in our heart things that we can cultivate and grow?

Is there someone in your life who is deeply spiritual, pious, or devout?

Have you ever visited a holy place?

How would your life benefit from a consistent expression of reverence?

OCTOBER 04

RIDING A BIKE

"Truly, the bicycle is the most influential piece of product design ever."

—Hugh Pearman

"Nothing compares to the simple pleasure of a bike ride."

—John F. Kennedy

A bike ride is a magical thing. It has the power to remove stress, improve your health, remind you of your childhood, and show you the world. Best of all, bikes are slow enough to let you see the world and wave hello along the way.

When was the last time you went for a bike ride?

Do you own a bike?

Are there bike trails and scenic rides near where you live?

What do you think of virtual bike rides that allow you stay at home but see the Pyrenees on your screen?

Have you ever considered joining a bike club, buying some spandex, and going hard-core cycling?

Do you have a cycling preference, like touring, mountain biking, racing, or casual pedaling?

Who would you like to invite to go on a bike ride?

How might the fun and exercise of going for a bike ride improve your quality of life?

OCTOBER 05

RIGHT BRAIN / LEFT BRAIN

"It's a left-brain right-brain thing. People are more agreeable toward people on their left."
—Michael Connelly

"Reading is more of a left-brain process, and listening to music is a right-brain function."
—Maynard James Keenan

Popular culture believes the world is divided into left-brain logical thinkers and right-brain creative thinkers. Although not scientifically true, it does help us understand how people prefer to interpret the world.

Do you believe there is value in making a distinction between right-brain thinkers and left-brain thinkers?

Are you right-brained or left-brained?

Would you agree that people generally perceive the world in these two distinct ways?

What are the benefits of being left-brained?

What are the benefits of being right-brained?

Do you have greater respect and value for one over the other?

Can you think of an example of how this distinction has helped you appreciate and understand someone?

Instead of forcing others to see the world from your own perspective, how can you open up and appreciate theirs?

RISK-TAKER

"Living with fear stops us taking risks, and if you don't go out on the branch, you're never going to get the best fruit."

—Sarah Parish

"In the end, what we regret most are the chances we never took."

—Fraiser Crane (Fraiser)

Risk-taking can be courageous or foolish depending on the outcome. A risk-taker values the possibility over the embarrassment. The risk-averse believe good possibilities don't require choosing between the two.

Are you a risk-taker?

How did you observe your parents avoiding or pursuing risk?

What is one risk you took that you are most proud of?

Is there a risk you took that ended in disaster?

Do you believe there are different categories of risk? How can we tell the difference?

What do you think of the phrase "the greater the risk, the greater the reward"?

Is there someone you know who took a risk and lost it all?

Do you believe your life would be better if you pursued more risk or pursued less risk?

RITES OF PASSAGE

"No longer a mark of distinction or proof of achievement, a college education is these days a mere rite of passage, a capstone to adolescent party time."
—William A. Henry III

"Every positive change, every jump to a higher level of energy and awareness involves a rite of passage. Each time to ascend to a higher rung on the ladder of personal evolution, we must go through a period of discomfort or initiation. I have never found an exception."
—Don Millman

Rites of passage remind us that we don't live life alone but in community. They remind us that where we are is where others have been. Rites of passage are just another way of saying, "Welcome to the club."

What are some modern-day rites of passage?

Have you marked your own rites of passage through a ceremony or celebration?

If you were to create a new rite of passage, what would it celebrate and how would it add value to someone's life?

Do you feel that some rites of passage are just a community's way to keep its members humble?

Have you ever had to endure an initiation period or hazing to become a member of a club or community?

How do our shared struggles and challenges unite us?

What is one way you can celebrate an important transition in the life of someone you love?

RITUALS

"Ritual is important to us as human beings. It ties us to our traditions and our histories."

—Miller Williams

"Rituals give kids a sense of security in a fast-moving, unpredictable world, as well as memories they will cherish a lifetime."

—Betsy Taylor

A ritual is a symbolic act that reenacts our story. OUR STORY is the meta-narrative that gives life meaning. Rituals remind us what's important in life, and we should all be required to create a few rituals of our own.

Do you have any rituals in your life?

How would you define a ritual? Does it need to have deep significance, or can it be a simple thing like brushing your teeth before bed?

Did your family have any unique, fun, or quirky rituals that you share together?

How can something like "pizza night" create an important ritual for a family or friends to share?

Do you practice any religious rituals, like observing the sacraments, fasting, or going on a pilgrimage?

Has society replaced sacred rituals for secular ones, like observing Super Bowl Sunday?

What are some ways you can express the important virtues and values in your life through a ritual of your own design?

ROAD TRIPS

"Road trips required a couple of things: a well-balanced diet of caffeine, salt, and sugar and an excellent selection of tunes—oh, and directions."
—Jenn McKinlay

"Life is too short to not go on that spontaneous road trip."
—Unknown

Most of us have a stage in our life when we have more time than money. Road trips don't represent a time efficient form of travel, but they represent a wonderful form of "knowing" that requires time.

Do you like to take road trips?

When was the last time you took a road trip?

When was the first time you took a road trip? Who was with you, in what car, and to what destination?

Have you ever taken a road trip without any specific destination?

If someone had the money to fly, how would you convince them to take a road trip instead?

What's the longest distance you've ever traveled by car?

When you take a road trip, is it important for you to take the back roads?

What would be the value of planning a major road trip with family or friends in the next year?

OCTOBER 10

ROMANCE

"Romance is dead—it was acquired in a hostile takeover by Hallmark and Disney, homogenized, and sold off piece by piece."

—Yeardly Smith

"Romance is everything."

—Gertrude Stein

The word *romance* was originally used to describe a type of story about a knight or hero. The concept of love didn't come until the late 17th century, but it's still brave and courageous to pursue another human being.

———————————————

Are you romantic?

How did your parents express romance in their marriage?

Do you have a favorite romantic comedy?

How have film and fantasy distorted the way we understand romance?

What are some things you consider to be truly romantic or demonstrate the pursuit of romance?

Do you believe people fall in love or find love at first sight?

Does romance take up a lot of your thought life?

Do you believe men and women think differently about romance?

How could a little more romance improve your life?

ROOMMATES

"A good roommate may be the single most important thing to have when one is away at school."
—Barbara Dana

"The people you live with at college, those first roommates, often are people you're still friends with the rest of your life."
—Richard Linklater

Most people who go to college are confronted with the reality of a roommate. Your first roommate is someone you'll never forget; they either become a lifelong friend or someone who helped you to grow.

———————————————

Do you currently have a roommate?

Who was your first roommate beyond sharing a bedroom with a sibling?

Do you still have a friendship today with someone who was once your roommate?

Did your college allow you to choose your roommate, or did they just assign roommates randomly?

What is the value of learning to share a room or small apartment with someone?

Were you guilty of being a messy or annoying roommate?

Would you prefer to live alone?

How is the relationship you have with a roommate different from a marriage relationship?

ROUTINE

"You'll never change your life until you change something you do daily. The secret to your success is found in your daily routine."

—John C. Maxwell

"The secret of your future is hidden in your daily routine."

—Mike Murdock

A routine can be a rut that bores you to death. It can also be a ritual that makes your dreams come true. How you think about a routine will put you in prison or set you on the road to freedom.

———————————————————

Do you like to have a routine?

Did your parents establish a daily routine for your family, and how strictly did they enforce it?

Have you ever felt trapped by routine?

So much of life is consumed by things we repeat every day; how can we break out of our daily routine?

Are you someone who thrives in the context of structure and routine?

Why is it important to give children structure and routine?

Have you ever used a timeline or hourly calendar to set up your schedule?

How could more structure and intentional routine improve your productivity and lower your stress?

OCTOBER 13
SACRIFICE

"Sacrifice is a part of life. It's supposed to be. It's not something to regret. It's something to aspire to."

—Mitch Albom

"Sacrifice is the essence of love, which is the essence of God."

—Rick Warren

Sacrifice is an ancient practice that required the slaughtering of a life to pay for sin. Today, sacrifice doesn't require blood but describes our willingness to suffer for the benefit of others and ourselves.

———————————————

Are you making sacrifices for something or someone?

How did your parents make sacrifices for you and your family?

Is making a sacrifice for your own benefit the same as making a sacrifice for someone else?

Does the biblical practice of sacrifice have any benefit for how we understand sacrifice today?

Is there one anyone you know who has given the ultimate sacrifice of their life to save someone else?

Is there a simple sacrifice you could make that would make a big difference?

How can you more fully embrace self-sacrifice as an expression of loving others?

SALARY

"To kill yourself for earning a salary is not worth it."

—Nargis Fakhri

"The more they applaud, the bigger your salary will be."

—Anna Held

The word *salary* comes from the Latin word for salt, because Roman soldiers were paid for their service with salt, which was then a valuable commodity. This is why we ask people today if they are "worth their salt."

Are you happy with the salary you earn?

Do you think your parents earned a salary that they were worth or content to receive?

Has an annual salary become one of the most significant ways we estimate someone's worth?

Do you live on a fixed salary, or does your income fluctuate every month?

How much money would you need to make annually to be content with your salary?

Do you believe that someone's salary is a secret never to be shared?

What is your current salary?

How can we begin to compensate and esteem people in other ways?

SANCTITY OF LIFE

"Instead of the traditional emphasis on the sanctity of life, bioethics began to stress the quality of life, meaning that many damaged humans, young and old, don't qualify for personhood because their lives have lost value."
—John Leo

"In the 21st century, I believe the mission of the United Nations will be defined by a new, more profound awareness of the sanctity and dignity of every human life, regardless of race or religion."
—Kofi Annan

The value we place on the sanctity of life is of great consequence. Make sure you value life in all its forms and conditions or someday you might find yourself on the list of a life to be discontinued.

Do you feel comfortable talking about the sanctity of life?

Have you ever had to discuss or debate the issues of abortion, mercy killing, or euthanasia?

Do you believe that taking another person's life can ever be justified?

Do you know anyone who refused to serve in the military because they held a strong position on the sanctity of life?

How can someone be so passionately opposed to abortion but so patriotically prepared to go to war?

How has the sanctity of life been instilled in you?

Does it concern you to think that there people who make decisions every day about who lives and who dies?

SARCASM

"Sarcasm is like cheap wine; it leaves a terrible aftertaste."

—Dana Perino

"Sarcasm I now see to be, in general, the language of the devil; for which reason I have long since as good as renounced it."

—Thomas Carlyle

Sarcasm is a witty and humorous way to convey contempt. On the outside, we use words that sound humorous, but on the inside we find nothing more than anger and disdain. It's not very attractive.

Do you find yourself being sarcastic?

Why do we see sarcasm as funny?

Are you able to recognize sarcasm when you hear it?

Is there a certain amount of sarcasm that you believe is harmless, like saying "Lovely weather we're having" when it's cold and rainy?

Why is it so popular to make fun of public figures, politicians, and movie stars through sarcasm?

Have you ever tried to remove sarcasm from you life?

Is there someone you know who is so good at sarcasm that you don't always know if they are speaking the truth or making a joke?

How can we keep each other accountable to avoid sarcasm?

SAVE THE CAT

"In a fire, between a Rembrandt and a cat, I would save the cat."

—Alberto Giacometti

"Save the what? I call it the 'save the cat' scene. It's the scene where we meet the hero and he does something that defines who he is and makes us, the audience, like him."

—Blake Snyder

Thanks, Blake Snyder, for introducing us to the concept of "save the cat." You want a better story? Take time to be kind and help others. It may seem counter-intuitive, but it's one of the best ways to get what you want.

Do you feel like the world is on your side?

How have you been motivated to help others because of the kindness you've observed in their life?

Have you observed the "save the cat" principle in the movies, and could you give an example?

Have you watched films where you didn't like the protagonist at first but were slowly convinced to change your opinion?

Are you the "good guy" in the story but feel like you're often seen as the opposite?

Is it important to "save the cat" when no one is watching?

How can you practice "save the cat" on a more consistent basis?

OCTOBER 18

SAVERS vs SPENDERS

"The quickest way to double your money is to fold it over and put it back in your pocket."

—Will Rogers

"Economy does not lie in sparing money but in spending it wisely."

—Thomas Henry Huxley

Savers vs spenders—another great topic to split the room. Spenders will argue, "You can't take it with you!" to which the savers respond, "I don't plan on leaving anytime soon, and my money needs to last."

———————————————

Are you a saver or a spender?

Were your parents savers or spenders?

Do you have several savings accounts, including an account for retirement?

What do you think about the financial principle that suggests you have one year's salary saved in the bank?

Do you know someone so obsessed with saving that they can't take a holiday or purchase a new car?

What is the most reckless, unwise purchase you've ever made?

Is it possible to have a healthy balance between saving and spending?

How can your saving and spending habits improve this year?

SCIENCE

"Science is simply the word we use to describe a method of organizing our curiosity."

—Tim Minchin

"What we know is a drop; what we don't know is an ocean."

—Isaac Newton

Science is the study of the nature and behavior of natural things. Its findings are to be based on objective data, and repeatable phenomenon, but how limited we are to explain the vastness of the universe.

Do you like science?

What was the last science class you took?

Is there a particular branch of science that interests or intrigues you?

Do you know anyone employed in a scientific field?

In what ways do you believe science has been a great benefit to world?

How is science guilty of imposing a story, interpretation, or an agenda on less than truly objective facts?

Do you have a favorite scientist or scientific discovery?

What is one way you can keep the scientist in you alive, growing, and discovering new things?

SCREEN TIME

*"I think it's necessary to let kids get bored once in a while—
that's how they learn to be creative."*

—Kim Raver

*"We're raising a generation of children who are
uncomfortable with building relationships directly and
prefer to have a screen between them and the world."*

—Cat Jennings

**The average daily screen time in America is over two
hours and in some cases over three. Attention spans
are declining, and people are less healthy and happy.
We are seeking to be perpetually amused.**

Are you aware how much time you spend each day looking
at your phone, computer, video game, or TV?

Did your parents monitor and control how much screen
time you had every day?

Do you currently use an app to monitor the amount of time
you spend daily on electronic devices?

Do you feel that having greater access to the world through
technology has improved our lives?

Do you have specific times during the day where you turn
off all electronic devices?

What is your greatest screen time obsession?

How can you create better screen time habits?

THE SECRET

"Thoughts become things. If you see it in your mind, you will hold it in your hand."

—Bob Proctor

"The Great Secret of Life is the law of attraction. The law of attraction can also be called the law of creation. In other words, life is not happening to you, you are creating it."

—Rhonda Byrne

In 2006, Rhonda Byrne wrote a book called *The Secret*. It has sold over 300 million copies and has been translated into 50 languages. The premise suggests we have the power to manifest whatever we desire.

―――――――――――――――――

Do you believe in the power of positive thinking?

Have you read *The Secret* or seen the film?

Are you someone who likes to read books or watch videos on self-help and self-improvement?

Do you have a favorite self-help guru?

What do you believe is the downside to the messages that suggest we can have anything we want in life?

Have you ever thought that the only ones that are getting rich and living their dreams are the people selling us on how to get them?

Is it possible positive thinking produces negative effects?

What do you believe is the secret to getting what you want out of life?

SELF-CONTROL

"What it lies in our power to do, it lies in our power not to do."

—Aristotle

"Self-control is one mark of a mature person; it applies to control of language, physical treatment of others, and the appetites of the body."

—Joseph B. Wirthlin

Self-control is the power to tell your body what to do, what to say, and what to think. It is staggering to consider what could be accomplished if we could only master these three things.

How would you describe your level of self-control?

Is there one area of your life where you a have high level of self-control?

Is there an area of your life where you continually struggle with self-control?

Have you ever had an episode where you lost all control and went berserk?

How does someone go about developing greater levels of self-control?

Is there one food, dessert, or recipe that challenges your self-control?

In which area would you like to increase your power of self-control: your actions, your words, or your thoughts?

What is one thing you like to start doing or stop doing?

SELF-IMAGE

"You have been criticizing yourself for years, and it hasn't worked. Try approving of yourself and see what happens."

—Louise L. Hay

"Be who you were created to be, and you will set the world on fire."

—St. Catherine of Sienna

Mirror, mirror on the wall, do I like what I see or not at all? To like yourself is a great advantage in life. There's nothing better than having a little voice in your head that cheers you up and cheers you on.

Do you have a positive self-image?

What are some things that people have said about the way you look that have stuck with you?

If you could change one thing about yourself, what would you change?

Are you more critical about how you look on the outside or on the inside?

Who has been the most positive influence on boosting your self-image?

Do you find yourself comparing the way you look and act to unrealistic people in magazines and movies?

What can you do in the next 30 days that will improve the way you think and feel about yourself?

SELF-IMPROVEMENT

"There is only one corner of the universe you can be certain of improving, and that's your own self."
—Aldous Huxley

"Those who cannot change their minds cannot change anything."
—George Bernard Shaw

Self-improvement is one of the largest sections of any bookstore. You can cut through them all with one question: "Does this book place 'self' at the center of the universe?" Remember: It's not about you.

———————————————

What does the phrase "It's not about you" mean?

Have you read many books on self-help and self-improvement?

What is the best advice anyone has given you that has helped you grow as a person?

Is there one area that is the focus of your need for self-improvement?

Is there one author, philosophy, or movement that has been especially helpful for you in the area of self-improvement?

Do you believe most people are consumed with themselves instead of the purpose and value they can offer to others?

What do you think about the phrase "When you lose your life, you'll find it".

Can you improve yourself by being less obsessed with yourself?

SELF-TALK

"Talk to yourself like you would to someone you love."

—Karolina Kurkova

"Instead of saying, 'I'm damaged, I'm broken, I have trust issues,' say, 'I'm healing, I'm rediscovering myself, I'm starting over.' "

—Horacio Jones

If we could only talk to ourselves the way we talk to a Little Leaguer playing baseball: "Come on, you can do it. Don't worry, you'll get a hit next time. A walk is as good as a hit. It's okay, everyone strikes out sometimes."

How would you describe the way you talk to yourself?

Have you ever had to tell yourself to shut up?

Are the words in your head just thoughts, or do you actually hear a voice in your mind?

How can you reprogram some of the negative messages in your head?

What is one thing you really like about yourself?

Do you have a verse, poem, or written meditation that helps you get to a better place?

Why do you think people are so hard on themselves when they would never speak to others the way they speak to themselves?

What is one positive message you can repeat to yourself again and again?

SERENITY

"Serenity: to be in a sense of inner peace, even in challenging situations."

—Lee Horbachewski

"Serenity comes when you trade expectations for acceptance."

—Unknown

We can thank *Seinfeld* for giving us Frank Costanza and his classic line "Serenity now!" How ironic to think we might be able to will peace and tranquility into our lives by shouting it into being.

Would you consider your life to be peaceful and serene?

How would you describe your home life and childhood? Was it peaceful and serene?

When was the last time you experienced an extended period of serenity?

Have you ever experienced *shalom*, the Hebrew word that includes all the feelings of wholeness, completeness, soundness, peace, safety, and prosperity?

Is there special place you go to pursue the quietness and restoration that comes with serenity?

How do the goals and pressures of life seem to contradict and combat the goals of serenity and shalom?

What are some tangible ways that you protect and produce the importance of serenity in your daily life?

SEX

"Sex is more than an act of pleasure; it's the ability to be able to feel so close to a person, so connected, so comfortable that it's almost breathtaking to the point you feel you can't take it. And at this moment, you're a part of them."

—Thom York

"Women need a reason to have sex. Men just need a place."

—Billy Crystal

The need for sex has produced and ended more marriages than you could ever imagine. Sex that emerges from deep love is sublime; sex that comes from selfishness will never be satisfied.

———————————————

Have you been able to form a healthy view toward sex?

How did you first learn about sex?

How has society turned sex into an obsession that is always in our face?

Why do you think sex is something that most couples fight about?

Do you think couples should wait to have sex until they are married?

What do you think is the secret to having a happy, healthy sex life for married couples, especially as they get older?

OCTOBER 28

SHOES

"Give a girl the right shoes, and she can conquer the world."

—Marilyn Monroe

"Men tell me that I've saved their marriages. It costs them a fortune in shoes, but it's cheaper than a divorce."

—Manolo Blahnik

You can tell a lot about a person by their shoes. Are they more concerned with fashion or comfort? Are they cheap, practical, or extravagant? All potential marriage partners should be required to explain their shoes.

_____

What shoes are you wearing?

Where did your parents take you to buy new shoes?

When was the first time you bought your own shoes and what did you buy?

Have you ever purchased an extravagant pair of shoes to make a statement?

How many pair of shoes do you currently own?

What are your favorite pair of shoes?

How much are you willing to pay for a pair of everyday work or school shoes?

Do you evaluate people by the shoes they wear? Do you believe that shoes can influence your career chances?

SILENCE

"Silence is true wisdom's best reply."

—Euripides

"Silence is one of the great arts of conversation."

—Cicero

People live in cities without silence; 24 hours a day, life is filled with the sound of sirens, honking horns, and street noise. Perhaps it's not physical silence we need to survive but the ability to turn off distraction.

———————————————

Do you crave silence?

Is there a place you can go that is free from noise and distraction?

Would you characterize your family as loud or quiet?

Do you believe long periods of silence might make you go crazy?

Have you ever experience long periods of silence from someone you loved?

Have you ever given someone the silent treatment?

Do you believe that silence is more than the absence of sound, or is it the absence of distraction?

What is one thing you can do to create a place of silence and experience time free from all distraction?

SIMPLICITY

"Simplicity is the ultimate sophistication."
—Leonardo da Vinci

"If you cannot explain it simply, you don't understand it well enough."
—Albert Einstein

Simplicity is the ability to enjoy something in its purest form. It is a core value of good design and a core virtue for life. Learning to appreciate life in its simplest form is to be truly free.

———————————————————

Would you consider your life to be complicated?

Do you miss the simplicity of childhood?

Has anyone you know ever pursued a minimalist approach to living?

How have we overly complicated our lives in America?

Have you ever considered "going off the grid" or pursuing a minimalist approach to life?

Is there something or someone that always seems to complicate your life?

What is one thing you could remove from your life that you wouldn't miss or even know was gone?

How can you pursue a life of simplicity in the next year? What things need to change or be removed?

SCARY THINGS

"Monsters are real; ghosts are real too. They live inside us, and sometimes, they win."

—Stephen King

"Shadows of a thousand years rise again unseen. Voices whisper in the trees, 'Tonight is Halloween!' "

—Dexter Kozen

Halloween is not about elaborate costumes or how much candy you can collect; it's about our imagination. Halloween gives us an opportunity to dress up and be whoever we want to be, even if it's scary.

Do you like Halloween?

When was the last time you put on a costume for Halloween, and what was it?

What was Halloween like in your neighborhood when you were growing up?

Did you make your own costumes, rent them, or buy them from the store?

What was your favorite Halloween costume ever?

Did you trick-or-treat, go to a party, or not celebrate Halloween at all?

Do you think there's something dark and evil about Halloween?

What is one way to make Halloween better for everyone?

SINCERITY

"Sincerity is the face of the soul."
　　　　　　　　　　　　　—Joseph Sanial-Dubay

"One of the most sincere forms of respect is actually listening to what another has to say."
　　　　　　　　　　　　　—Bryant H. McGill

The word *sincerity* comes from two Latin words, and literally means "without wax." Less-than-honest sculptors were known to hide their mistakes and flaws by filling cracks and imperfections with wax.

Would you consider yourself to be sincere?

Have you ever been deceived by someone who led you to believe they were telling the truth?

Have you ever been in a situation where you were pressured to go along with the crowd and you didn't feel like you could be honest and sincere?

Who is a friend that you can always count on to be genuine and sincere?

Are you someone who can see through people when they are being less than honest?

Do you believe there are times when it's better to tell people what they want to hear?

How can you become more sincere as you interact with the people in your life?

SINGING

"Those who wish to sing always find a song."

—Swedish Proverb

"I want to sing like the birds sing, not worrying about who hears or what they think."

—Rumi

Singing is good for the soul. It physically changes your disposition and opens your heart to joy. Figure out how and where to sing without fear or inhibition. When you sing, your brain tells your body, "I'm happy!"

————————————————————

Do you like to sing?

Did your family sing or was there music in your home?

Have you ever had the opportunity to sing in public?

Do you know if you're a soprano, alto, tenor, or bass?

Who is your favorite professional singer?

Do you have a place where you feel free to sing without being judged?

Have you ever gone with a group of friends to sing karaoke?

Do you have a friend or family member who thinks they're a good singer but they're not?

Are you perfectly happy to go through life without singing, or do you believe more singing could be a good thing?

SLEEP

"A good laugh and a long sleep are the two best cures for anything."

—Irish Proverb

"I love sleep. My life has the tendency to fall apart when I'm awake, you know?"

—Ernest Hemingway

Sleep allows your body to repair itself and prepare for a new day. Sleep allows your mind to purge and recharge. Sleep is an act of kindness to yourself and to everyone you meet the next day.

———————————————

How much sleep to get each night?

When do you usually go to bed?

Are you a light sleeper or a deep sleeper?

Have you ever used sleeping pills or medicine to help you sleep?

What's the longest you've ever gone without sleep?

Do you usually have dreams or nightmares?

Do you have a nighttime routine before going to bed?

How hard is it for you to wake up in the morning?

Would you consider yourself a night person or a morning person?

Could better sleep improve the quality of your life?

NOVEMBER 04

SOCIAL MEDIA

"Don't believe everything you read in books or on the Internet just because someone makes up a quote and puts their name next to it."

—Mark Twain

"Social media has created jealous behavior over illusions. Sadly, some are envious of things, relationships, and lifestyles that don't even exist."

—Unknown

Social media is a pervasive and powerful influence on the way we understand the world. The challenge is no longer knowing how to use social media but having the discernment to determine its worth.

Are you addicted to social media?

What social media platforms do you use?

Are there some social media platforms you refuse to use or have deleted from your devices?

What do you think about social media platforms having the power to "turn off" voices they don't agree with?

Do you believe your life is better because of social media?

How many minutes a day do you think you devote to social media?

Do you believe every generation will have their own preferred social media platforms and expressions?

How can you develop a more healthy social media practice that demonstrates balance and discernment?

SOLITUDE

"Solitude is fine, but you need someone to tell that solitude is fine."

—Honoré de Balzac

"Without great solitude, no serious work is possible."

—Pablo Picasso

When solitude is a choice, it's considered a treat and a reward. When solitude is forced upon us, it's considered extreme punishment. It's our ability to choose when we experience solitude that makes the difference.

Do you pursue times of solitude?

Have you ever been punished by being forced to be alone?

What's the longest amount of time that you have ever been alone?

What do you think might be the value of spending an extended amount of time alone like a hermit in the desert?

How would you cope with being sentenced to solitary confinement?

Do you believe it's important to find a place to be alone?

Have you ever felt alone in a crowd?

How might pursuing times of solitude bring good things?

SONGS

"There were times in life that the only thing I had was a song, and it carried me."

—Unknown

"Words make you think a thought. Music makes you feel a feeling. A song makes you feel a thought."

—E. Y. Harburg

Songs are the soundtracks of our lives. We have songs that take us back to high school, songs that remind us of falling in love. Our favorite songs produce emotions we once felt and help us feel them all over again.

What's your favorite song?

Is there one song that reminds you of high school?

Are there songs your mom and dad played that always take you "back home"?

Is there one song that sticks in your head and you sing it all day?

Have you ever created a playlist of songs for a friend?

Do you have a special song that you share with someone?

What are some of your favorite bands?

What does your music collection say about you?

SOULMATES

"A soulmate is someone who has locks that fit our keys, and keys that fit our locks."
—Richard Bach

"You walked into my life like you had always lived there, like my heart was a home built just for you."
—A. R. Asher

To marry your soulmate is a blissful thought. But it's more likely you'll marry someone who thinks and feels differently than you. Just remember this—the highest expression of romance is that two distinct souls would spend 50+ years learning to unite themselves into one.

Do you believe in soulmates?

Have you found your soulmate?

Is the notion of finding your soulmate nothing more than a selfish desire to be with someone like yourself?

What would be the advantage of being with someone who agreed with you and understood you completely?

Is there evidence that soulmates exist based on the relationships you have observed?

Do you believe movies and romance novels perpetuate the obsession we have with finding our soulmate?

Can you describe the qualities of your soulmate?

If life is hard and marriage is hard, how can you grow to become a more understanding partner?

SPECULATION

"Speculation is not knowledge."

—Robert M. Price

"There are two times in a man's life when he should not speculate—when he can't afford it and when he can."

—Mark Twain

Speculation is often associated with taking a financial risk, but it can also describe any decision that is based on feelings and not the facts. It may seem obvious to always go with the facts, but there are thousands of success stories born from an irrational hunch.

Do you make decisions based on speculation?

How would you define the word *speculation*?

Have you ever had a strong feeling in your gut that something was going to happen?

How do you respond to people when they promote or defend their decisions based on their feelings?

Do you take risks with your money and speculate on investments or financial opportunities?

When was the last time you made a decision based on speculation?

What's the biggest decision you've ever made without having all the facts?

Do you think you should speculate more or less?

SPORTS

"Sports do not build character. They reveal it."
—Heywood Broun

"Sports teaches you character, it teaches you to play by rules, it teaches you to know what it feels like to win and lose—it teaches you about life."
—Billie Jean King

Sports are a great metaphor for life. They teach you how to win and lose. They force you to prepare, focus, and pursue a goal. You learn to play as a team and work together. And, just like life, sports can be fun!

Do you like sports?

Did you play on a sports team when you were young?

What are your favorite sports to play?

Do you have a favorite team or teams that you support?

How often do you watch sports on TV?

Do you like to get together with friends to watch big sporting events, like the Superbowl, the World Series, or the Olympics?

Is there a sports fanatic in your life who is always talking about the players, the stats, and last night's game?

Would you rather watch or play sports?

How can you use athletic competition to improve your life?

STARGAZING

"Looking at the sky full of stars, she smiled. I thought she was stargazing, little did I know that's how she spoke to her parents."

—Caryl Rodrigues

"Look up at the stars, not down at your feet."

—Stephen Hawking

Stargazing implies much more than an interest in astronomy and the universe. It is a fascination with those things we see but never really know. Stargazing is wonder, awe, and the possibility of more.

Do you like to look at the stars?

Did you ever own a telescope?

Can you identify any constellations?

Have you ever spent a night waiting to see a comet, shooting star, or eclipse?

Have you had the opportunity to observe the stars from a different hemisphere?

Do you live in a place where you can see many stars?

Are you a romantic stargazer?

When was the last time you went stargazing?

What are the benefits of contemplating the galaxy and all it contains?

NOVEMBER 11

MILITARY SERVICE

*"We sleep soundly in our beds because rough men stand
ready in the night to visit violence on those who would do
us harm."*
—Winston Churchill

*"I only regret that I have but one life to give for my
country."*
—Nathan Hale

Veterans Day evolved from Armistice Day, which
marked the end of World War I. Today, we pause to
celebrate all the men and women who have served to
defend our country. Remember to stop a veteran and
say, "Thank you for your service."

————————————

Are you taking any time today to celebrate Veterans Day?

Did anyone in your family serve in the military?

Are there picnics and parades in your community to
celebrate our veterans?

Do you live in a part of the USA where the military and
military service are celebrated?

Were you ever a soldier, or have you ever considered
military service?

Do you believe our country does enough to celebrate and
provide for our veterans?

Should military service be mandatory for everyone in our
country like it is in so many others?

STORIES

"Stories create community, enable us to see through the eyes of other people, and open us to the claims of others."

—Peter Forbes

"Storytelling is the most powerful way to put ideas into the world today."

—Robert McKee

There was a time when people would say, "Stop telling stories." Stories carried the stigma of a lie, a fib, or an outlandish tale meant to deceive or embellish. Today, stories are considered the basis for understanding life.

Are you a storyteller?

Did you grow up listening to your parents and grandparents telling the stories from their lives?

What's one story from your life that you tell over and over again?

Do you have a tendency to embellish the facts on some of your stories?

Who is the best storyteller you know?

Why do you think stories have become the basis for establishing brand identity and marketing?

How do your stories identify who you are, what you believe, and what you want out of life?

SUCCESS

"Success isn't always about greatness. It's about consistency. Consistent hard work leads to success. Greatness will come."

—Dwayne Johnson

"If you focus on success, you'll have stress, but if you pursue excellence, success will be guaranteed."

—Deepak Chopra

Success will determine your level of contentment and satisfaction with life. You should never be satisfied or content with failure and defeat. Just remember that it's up to you to decide what "success" means.

What is your definition of success?

Would you consider yourself to be successful?

How did your parents measure success, and do you measure up?

How does society measure success, and how does your definition differ?

Is there one goal, achievement, or dollar amount that defines success for you?

Do you spend a lot of time thinking about being successful and trying to figure out ways to get ahead?

How would a different definition of success set you up for a life of contentment?

SUMMER VACATION

"When all else fails, take a vacation."

—Betty Williams

"A vacation is having nothing to do and all day to do it in."

—Robert Orben

Summer vacations are the delight of every child: 100 days of freedom to just be a kid and learn the things they don't teach at school, like catching fireflies, building sandcastles, climbing trees, and making s'mores.

Do you have fond memories of your summer vacations?

Did your family go camping, visit family, or take trips around the country for summer vacation?

When was the last time you took a vacation, and where did you go?

Do vacations have to be in the summer?

How long are your vacations, and how much do you spend?

Is there one summer that you'll always remember?

What are the things that define summer for you?

Do you have any special plans for the upcoming summer?

How can setting time aside to pursue rest and relaxation be life-giving for you and your family?

SUPERPOWERS

"The things that make us different, those are our superpowers."

—Lena Waithe

"You don't need superpowers to be someone's hero."

—Ricky Maye

If life is a story and you are the hero, then what is your superpower? A superpower doesn't have to be something supernatural; it can be anything you do that produces goodness, beauty, or truth.

Do you have a favorite superhero or superpower?

How has the superhero myth influenced our understanding of life and its purpose?

Do you consider yourself to be a hero who defends and protects something good, beautiful, or true?

What is one skill or ability that makes you uniquely qualified to fight evil?

Do you know anyone who is into cosplay or obsessed with superheroes and villains?

Is there someone in your life who has been your hero?

What is the unique talent or ability that you need to start using for the benefit of others?

THE SUPERNATURAL

"The sea is only the embodiment of a supernatural and wonderful existence."

—Jules Verne

"Christianity is either supernatural or nothing at all."

—Reinhard Bonnke

A life beyond this one can be difficult for some to consider. But with all the books and films about the supernatural, it's hard to imagine going through life without having a few "What ifs?"

———————————————

Do you believe in the supernatural?

Do you believe in God?

Have you ever had an encounter with the supernatural?

What do you think of people who say they have had out-of-body experiences?

It is one thing to believe in God, but do you also believe in demons, angels, heaven, and hell?

What do you think happens when we die?

Do you believe in ghosts?

What is your thinking about the supernatural and the possibility of a metaphysical world?

SURPRISES

"Surprise is the greatest gift which life can grant us."

—Boris Pasternak

"There is no surprise more magical than the surprise of being loved: It is God's finger on man's shoulder."

—Charles Morgan

Some people love surprises, and it's hard for them to think anyone wouldn't. But the reality is some people think surprises are a cruel joke. They believe the good things in life are best enjoyed through thoughtful anticipation.

Do you like surprises?

Has anyone ever thrown you a surprise party, and did you enjoy it?

Is there one surprise in your life you'll never forget?

Do you have a friend or family member who is opposed to surprises?

Is there a difference between a good surprise and a bad one?

Why do people like stories with a surprise ending?

Is there value in learning how to appreciate a surprise?

Do you believe you need to spend more time preparing for life's surprises or learning to embrace them?

SUSPENSE

"Even cowards can endure hardship; only the brave can endure suspense."

—Mignon McLaughlin

"Suspense combines curiosity with fear and pulls them up a rising slope."

—Mason Cooley

Suspense requires uncertainty, and uncertainty always creates drama. Drama may make for a good story, but it doesn't always make for a stress-free life. In real life, it's nice to count on things, like getting paid.

Do you like being in suspense?

Are you a fan of suspense thriller movies?

Have you ever purposefully kept people in suspense?

Was there ever a time where you were waiting for big news to come and it was driving you crazy?

Many people wish their lives were more exciting, but how might it be better to have a life free of suspense?

Do you cope well with a pending unknown?

Is there something in your life right now that has you in suspense?

What's one thing you can do this year to add or remove the drama of suspense in your life?

SYMBOLS & SIGNS

"Symbols are powerful because they are the visible signs of invisible realities."

—St. Augustine

"Nature speaks in symbols and in signs."

—John Greenleaf Whittier

Symbols and signs are the images we use to represent our story. We assign meaning to an object that signifies a virtue or value. When we paste it on our wall or wear it on our t-shirt, we are reminded of what we believe.

———————————

Are there symbols or signs that are important to you?

Do you have any signs or symbols on your walls or on the bumper of your car?

Are there any symbols or signs that make you run the other way?

How have signs and symbols been used to create logos and brands, and which ones have caught your eye?

Do you practice a religion that has a long history of symbols and signs?

Have you ever created your own symbol or sign, and what does it mean?

How could a properly placed symbol help you remember something important?

Have you ever received a "sign" to do something?

TAKING TESTS

"I have failed my exam in some subjects, but my friend passed. Now he's an engineer in Microsoft, and I am the owner."
—Bill Gates

"When you do exams, you never want to be the one who finishes first, and you never want to be the one who finishes last."
—Anthony T. Hincks

A test is a tool used to evaluate what you know. Some tests require memorization. Other tests measure the ability to repeat a skill. The greatest test is life itself, which requires not only knowledge but wisdom.

Are you good at taking tests and exams?

What is the longest time you've ever devoted in preparation for an exam?

How well did you do on the ACT or other college entrance exams?

Have you ever been physically ill or lost sleep the night before an exam?

Do you believe that most of the information we memorize for an exam is quickly forgotten?

Have you ever taken an exam that was extremely practical and represents information you still use today?

How are the "tests" of daily life different from the exams you take at school?

NOVEMBER 21

TALENT

*"I really believe that everyone has a talent, ability, or skill
that he can mine to support himself and to succeed in life."*

—Dean Koontz

"Talent can't be taught, but it can be awakened."

—Wallace Stegner

The word *talent* is usually used to describe a natural skill or aptitude. Talent should produce gratitude instead of pride. For some reason God gave you a gift, and it's your job to give it back.

Were you born with a special talent?

Did anyone ever tell you when you were a child that you had a gift or that you had talent?

Was there someone in your family who seemed to be exceptionally gifted?

Is there one talent that you believe you have been able to cultivate and grow?

Is there a talent you wish you had?

Are you guilty of comparing your skills and abilities with other people?

Do you believe natural talent comes with an obligation?

How can you identify your talents and learn to use them for the benefit of others?

GRATEFULNESS

"Thankfulness is the beginning of gratitude. Gratitude is the completion of thankfulness. Thankfulness may consist merely of words. Gratitude is shown in acts."

—Henri Frederic Amiel

"Feeling gratitude and not expressing it is like wrapping a present and not giving it."

—William Arthur Ward

Thanksgiving is more than turkey and football. Gratefulness is a sure sign of mental and emotional stability. It is a clear indication that we know life is a gift. So find a creative way to say "thank you" every day.

What are your plans for Thanksgiving?

What are you grateful for today?

Is expressing gratitude a consistent and regular practice in your life?

To whom do you owe the most?

What are some great ways to show gratitude without using words?

Are you thankful to God?

Is there someone you should call and thank?

How does practicing gratitude affect our disposition?

How can you live a more grateful life?

TALKING ON THE PHONE

"Our most meaningful conversations go on late at night when we're on the phone with our friends or talking to our lovers."
—Marianne Williamson

"It's getting harder and harder to differentiate between schizophrenics and people talking on a cell phone. It still brings me up short to walk by somebody who appears to be talking to themselves."
—Bob Newhart

It won't be long before someone figures out how to implant a phone in our bodies. Here's to the brave few who have learned to put their phones down and choose to connect with humanity face-to-face.

Do you enjoy talking on the phone, or would you rather talk in person?

How much time do you spend talking on the phone every day?

Is it common for you to have a phone conversation that lasts more than an hour?

How many of your most important relationships are with people who live in a different city, state, or country?

How has the phone improved your relationships, and how has the phone been harmful?

Are you happy with the amount of time you spend talking on the phone, or would you like to make some changes?

TATTOOS

"Tattoos have a power and magic all their own. They decorate the body, but they also enhance the soul."

—Michelle Delio

"My body is my journal, and my tattoos are my story."

—Johnny Depp

Tattoos are controversial because they are permanent, but despite any negatives, tattoos are more popular than ever. Here's a great way to start a conversation— ask, "Would you tell me about your tattoo?"

Do you have a tattoo?

How did your parents feel about you getting a tattoo?

Is there a message, sign, or symbol that you believe is worth having permanently scribed on your skin?

Would you allow your children to get a tattoo, and if so, at what age?

Do you know where to go to get a tattoo and how much it costs?

Are you currently considering a tattoo?

Do you judge people by the quantity and content of their tattoos?

How could a tattoo add meaning to your life by making a statement about a relationship or life-changing event?

TECHNOLOGY

"Technology is a useful servant but a dangerous master."

—Christian L. Lange

"The purpose of technology is not to confuse the brain but to serve the body."

—William S. Burroughs

Technology represents more than electronics and computers. *Technology* is a word broad enough to include any device or application that solves a problem and makes life easier, which is great until technology itself becomes the problem.

———————————

Are you fascinated by technology?

Did your family embrace new technology as it became available?

Have you had any interest in pursuing a career in a technological field?

What are some of the most significant improvements technology has made in modern society?

What concerns you most about new advances in technology, and do you believe it needs to be legislated?

Are there some forms of technology you believe are unethical?

How can you be more aware of how technology is influencing your life both positively and negatively?

TELEVISION

"I find television very educating. Every time somebody turns on the set, I go into the other room and read a book."

—Groucho Marx

"Television is chewing gum for the eyes."

—Frank Lloyd Wright

Many people like to demonize television. For others, it's a window to the world that opens our minds to bigger things. It teaches us how to dream.

—————————————————

Do you like to watch television?

How many minutes do you watch television a week?

What television shows did you watch as a kid?

Did your parents control how much TV you watched?

How many televisions do you own?

Are you currently watching a TV series or binge watching a TV show online?

What do you think are some of the best TV shows of all time?

Is television as bad as they say it is?

How can you be more intentional about what you watch on television?

TELLING JOKES

"I don't make jokes. I just watch the government and report the facts."

—Will Rogers

"The best ideas come as jokes. Make your thinking as funny as possible."

—David Ogilvy

Everyone should have a good, clean joke ready to share when the moment arises. Life is filled with awkward moments, and there's nothing like a good joke to remind us not to take ourselves too seriously.

———————————————

Are you good at telling jokes?

Can you tell me a good joke right now?

What does it mean that "Telling a joke is all about timing"?

Where do you get your jokes? Do you own any joke books?

Do you have a favorite stand-up comedian?

Do you believe it's possible to be really funny without using off-color humor?

Have you ever considered trying out stand-up comedy at a local club?

What types of humor make you laugh?

Is there someone who needs you to tell them a joke?

TEMPTATION

"I can resist everything except temptation."

—Oscar Wilde

"Lead me not into temptation; I can find the way myself."

—Rita Mae Brown

The reality of temptation seems to argue for the existence of some form of cosmic drama. The world would be a different place if we all secretly fantasized about eating vegetables or struggled to fight back the urge to go for a run.

Do you struggle with temptation?

What tempts you?

Do you ever feel like "the devil made you do it"?

Have you ever considered why bad things are easy to do and good things require a strong will?

Have you ever had the opportunity to hold someone accountable for something?

Is temptation an outdated idea that just gives people an excuse or alibi for their mistakes?

What is something bad that you've been successful to avoid?

Regardless of what you think about temptation, where do you get the willpower to do what is right?

THAT CAME OUT WRONG

"When you think you have made a mistake, think of it as an opportunity to make something beautiful!"

—Barney Saltzberg

"We're petrified of saying too much or saying it wrong. When the truth is the only wrong thing you can say is nothing at all."

—Jackson Avery (*Grey's Anatomy*)

How wonderful it would be to live life with a 30-second delay. Think of how many times you said something wrong and you knew it the second after you said it. You would never have to say, "Well, that came out wrong."

Do you find it easy to come up with the right words?

Do you have an embarrassing story where the words just came out wrong?

Is there a situation or person that makes you nervous and causes you to say awkward things?

Have you ever left an awkward voicemail and wished you had a chance to erase it and leave a new one?

Have you ever experienced a Freudian slip?

Does it bother you when people use the wrong word or use words incorrectly?

Is there one conversation you wish you could erase?

How can you be more careful with your words?

THREE WISHES

"If I had Aladdin's lamp and the usual three wishes, the first would always be, 'Give me the first day of June!'"

—Gladys Taber

"The three wishes of every man: to be healthy, to be rich by honest means, and to be beautiful."

—Plato

There's an old saying, "If wishes were horses, beggars would ride." Certainly, no one should wish their life away, but you can learn a lot about someone by giving them three wishes.

Have you ever imagined what your three wishes would be?

Does it seem worthless to have wishes?

What were some of your dreams and wishes as a child?

Do you believe that the first step to achieving any goal is to imagine it?

What would it mean for your dreams to come true?

Has anyone ever trusted you enough to share their dreams with you?

Why are we so hesitant and timid to verbalize our dreams and what we want from life?

How can you be more honest about the dreams you have for your life and start figuring out how to pursue them?

THRIFTINESS

"It is thrifty to prepare today for the wants of tomorrow."

—Aesop

"Those who spend too much will eventually be owned by those who are thrifty."

—John Templeton

We rarely use the word *thrifty* anymore. We use it now to describe the quirky side of frugality, like someone who stuffs money in a mattress or collects pennies in a jar. Thriftiness simply means to be smart with money.

Would you consider yourself to be thrifty?

How would you define the word *thrifty*, and would you consider it to be a positive trait?

Were your grandparents and parents careful with their money?

Do you buy in bulk?

How much time do you spend researching ways to get the best deal and the lowest price?

Does making a major purchase paralyze you?

How much money do you need to have in the bank to feel safe?

What are some ways you can use your money more wisely?

TOUCH

"No other form of communication is as universally understood as touch. The compassionate touch of a hand or a reassuring hug can take way our fears, soothe our anxieties, and fill the emptiness of being lonely."

—Randi G. Find

"Touch comes before sight, before speech. It is the first language, and the last, and it always tells the truth."

—Margaret Atwood

Never underestimate the power of a hug. In a world so virtually and electronically connected, it's not uncommon for people to live without being touched or having any physical contact with another human being.

———————————

When was the last time you had a hug?

Are you someone who needs lots of physical contact, or are you happy with only what's necessary?

Do you believe that technology, with all its benefits, actually produces more distance and human separation?

Did you grow up in a family that expressed affection through physical touch?

How do you feel about all the social protocols and taboos that keep us from touching one another?

Is there someone in your life who gets very little human contact?

How can you use physical touch to encourage someone?

TRAVELING ABROAD

"Nobody can discover the world for somebody else. Only when we discover it for ourselves does it become common ground and a common bond and we cease to be alone."

—Wendell Berry

"One's destination is never a place, but a new way of seeing things."

—Henry Miller

Everyone should have the chance to experience life in another country, preferably one that uses another language. It is a form of poverty to see life only through the perspective of our own little world.

Have you had the chance to travel to another country?

How many countries have you visited outside of your own?

Have you studied another language, and does that influence where you want to travel?

Do you have a passport? When did you get one?

Is there one place in the world you would love to visit?

Do you think it's sad that people want to travel to other countries when they haven't explored their own?

What are the benefits of experiencing another country?

Are there any places you would be afraid to go?

How can you expand your appreciation for the world?

TRIBES

"When you find people who not only tolerate your quirks
but celebrate them with glad cries of 'Me too!' be sure to
cherish them. Because those weirdos are your tribe."

—Nenea Hoffman

"People aren't social. They're tribal. Race doesn't exist,
but tribes are real."

—Mat Johnson

Tribe is a word that comes from the field of anthropology
and is used to describe a people group or clan. Seth
Godin's book *Tribes* argues that modern tribes are the
result of our shared values, interests, and hobbies.

———————————————

Do you know anyone who has a family connection to a
traditional tribe or people group?

Why is it important to preserve and protect the culture and
customs of traditional tribes and clans?

With the onset of globalization, how have the concepts of
tribe and belonging changed?

Would you identify yourself as a member of a modern-day
tribe?

What are some of your values, interests, or hobbies that
draw you to a group of people who share the same?

Do you believe it is important to belong to a tribe, group, or
community?

What do we lose when we choose our community based on
mutual interests instead of physical proximity?

TROPHIES

"If everyone is special, then no one is. If everyone gets a trophy, trophies become meaningless."

—David McCullough

"You earn your trophies at practice. You just pick them up at the competitions."

—Unknown

Trophies, medals, and ribbons represent the triumphs and victories of life. They remind us that we were once strong and that this life can be conquered, at least for a brief time.

Do you have a collection of trophies, medals, and ribbons?

What victory are you most proud of?

What do you think of the "everyone gets a trophy" movement?

How has competition influenced your life?

When you were a child, did you like to see who could run the fastest, climb the highest, or throw the farthest?

Did you ever want to win an Olympic gold medal?

What would you like us to do with all your trophies, medals, and ribbons when you die?

How can you place the value of winning and the pride of victory in a healthy perspective?

TV SHOWS

"All TV shows are like cigarettes. You watch two, you have a higher chance of watching three. They're all addictive."

—Dan Harmon

"Today, watching television often means fighting, violence and foul language—and that's just deciding who gets to hold the remote control."

—Donna Gephart

There is something special about watching a TV series as it unfolds week to week. It's something to look forward to, and something to talk about in between. TV shows identify and unite a generation.

Do you have a favorite TV show?

How do you watch television—broadcast or on demand?

Did your family have a favorite TV show you watched together?

What were some of the most popular TV shows you've watched over the years?

Do you believe that TV shows are getting better in quality or worse?

Have you ever watched soap operas?

What genres or types of TV shows interest you most?

Do you have a healthy television habit, do you binge-watch, or is television non-existent in your life?

UNFULFILLED DREAMS

"Cemeteries are full of unfulfilled dreams ... countless echoes of 'could have' and 'should have' ... Don't choose to walk the well-worn path to regret."

—Steve Maraboli

"It's unfulfilled dreams that keep you alive."

—Robert H. Schuller

It has been said that the troubles of a child can be traced back to the unfulfilled dreams of their parents. Our disillusionment with life carries a heavy price tag that is often paid by others.

Do you have a dream for your life that would be hard to see go unfulfilled?

Do you think it's better to have smaller dreams and reach them or outlandish dreams and die trying?

What are some dreams your parents desired but never achieved?

How do you respond to the disappointment of not getting what you want?

Who is someone you admire for their ambition and big dreams?

Is it time for you to add some new dreams to fulfill?

How can you make sure you don't become disillusioned with life and keep pursuing your dreams?

UNIQUENESS

"What sets you apart can sometimes feel like a burden, and it's not. And a lot of the time, it's what makes you great."

—Emma Stone

"Always remember that you are absolutely unique. Just like everybody else."

—Margaret Head

No two snowflakes are exactly alike. You may be unique, but that in itself is not worthy of praise. Seek to be unique in your effort to accomplish good things. It will inspire others to pursue the same.

Is it important for you to be unique?

How have you been told that you are special and exceptional?

Did your family celebrate the uniqueness of each member, or were you encouraged to be the same?

Is uniqueness a Western value that promotes individualism unlike the Eastern values of conformity?

Do you own anything that is rare or valuable because it is one of a kind?

What do people pursue when they seek to purchase an original, one-of-a-kind object?

Is there someone you could encourage by pointing out a unique quality they possess?

How can you pursue uniqueness without producing pride?

VACATIONS

"Happiness consists of living each day as if it were the first day of your honeymoon and the last day of your vacation."

—Leo Tolstoy

"A vacation is what you take when you can longer take what you've been taking."

—Carl Wilson

Vacations have come to hold many meanings that extend far beyond rest and relaxation. Vacations are a status symbol, a statement of good taste, and an expression of who we are.

Do you ever feel pressure to go on an impressive vacation?

How did your family think about vacations, and what did they look like?

Where did you go on your last vacation?

Do you enjoy vacations that focus on rest and relaxation or vacations that focus on adventure?

Where are you planning to go on your next vacation?

Is it better for you to have fewer vacations for a longer time or multiple, short vacations?

Do you like to return to the same place every year or visit new destinations?

How can you pursue vacations more strategically in the future?

VICES

"The problem with people who have no vices is that generally, you can be pretty sure they're going to have some pretty annoying virtues."

—Elizabeth Taylor

"Men are more easily governed through their vices than through their virtues."

—Napoleon Bonaparte

Vices are bad habits and are measured by degree. Vices that are criminal, taboo, and immoral have the power to put us in jail. Other vices, like coffee, sleeping late, and chocolate, unite us through our shared weakness.

Do you have any vices?

Have you seen someone be controlled by their vices?

How would a vice be different than an addiction?

Did your parents have bad habits you might consider vices?

What are some vices you would consider to be acceptable, and which ones cross the line?

Have you ever smoked or been addicted to nicotine?

Is there one vice that concerns you or that you find especially annoying?

What is one habit or weakness you should re-evaluate as a negative behavior or vice?

VICTORY

"Victory belongs to the most persevering."

—Napoleon Bonaparte

"The harder the job is, the more beautiful the victory is."

—Franky Zapata

Victory is sweet, especially when you conquer yourself. Learn to defeat your laziness, your pride, your weaknesses, and your lack of discipline. Victory has more honor when you defeat yourself, not other team.

What has been one of your sweetest victories?

Is there an area of your life where you feel constantly defeated?

Have you ever been a member of a championship team?

Are you a sore loser?

Are you a humble winner?

Do you currently compete in a sport or activity?

What victory would represent your life's highest goal?

Have you learned to celebrate the small victories in your life?

How can you pursue more victories in your life without seeking to make other people losers?

VIDEO GAMES

"Video games are bad for you? That's what they said about rock and roll."
—Shigeru Miyamoto

"Some people say video games rot your brain, but I think they work different muscles that maybe you don't normally use."
—Ezra Koenig

There are billions of video gamers around the world, and the average age is 34. The gaming industry is expected to reach $180 billion with no signs of slowing down. It can also be argued they develop some important skills.

Do you like video games?

What was the first video game you ever played?

Did your parents see the value of video games, or did they think it was a waste of time?

Nintendo, Xbox, or Playstation?

How much money do you have invested in your video game system and software?

How many hours a week do you play video games?

What is your favorite video game of all time?

Have you ever thought about designing your own video game?

Is there a downside to video games?

VOICE

"I have always believed that when you have a voice, you have an obligation to use that voice to empower others."

—Diane von Furstenberg

"It only takes one voice, at the right pitch, to start an avalanche."

—Dianna Hardy

Voice can mean the sound you make when you're speaking or singing, but *voice* is often used to describe something more. Your voice is the unique message, style, or expression you bring to the things you do.

———————————————

Do you like the sound of your own voice?

Do you have a good singing voice?

What does it mean to give a voice to the voiceless?

Do you believe your voice is being heard and considered at the place you work or go to school?

How would you describe your personal style or unique expression?

Are there some creatives who have impressed you with their voice?

Why is it important to have your own voice and pursue a genuine expression of who you are?

How can you develop your own voice and the voice of others?

WEAKNESS

"Pain is weakness leaving the body."

—Chesty Puller

"Sometimes you don't realize your own strength until you come face to face with your greatest weakness."

—Susan Gale

The first step to working on our weaknesses is the awareness of what they are. The good news is that our weaknesses don't have to be a life sentence; they're more like muscles that need dumbbells and exercise.

What is your greatest weakness?

How have you discovered areas of weakness in your life?

Are you open about your weaknesses, or are they something you hide?

What's one thing you considered a weakness but has turned into a strength?

Would you define weakness as the absence of strength?

Have you ever had the opportunity to help someone work on weakness?

Have you ever worked out with weights to build muscle?

How can you embrace your weaknesses as an opportunity to grow?

WEDDINGS

"Many people spend more time in planning the wedding than they do in planning the marriage."

—Zig Ziglar

"If I cry at my wedding, it'll be because I'm overjoyed that the planning is finally over."

—Unknown

Weddings require you to make a million decisions. You have to decide on flowers, a cake, bridesmaid dresses, and a wedding gown. All of these decisions are easier if you've decided to marry the right person.

———————————————————

Are you married or do you plan to be?

How would you describe your wedding?

What was/will be the venue for your wedding?

What did/will the bridal party wear?

What was/will be the music at your wedding?

Did you/will you have a big party, dance, and DJ after the ceremony?

Who was/will be the officiant at your wedding, and what do you want them to say?

Did you/will you have a big wedding?

How much money is a reasonable amount to spend on a wedding?

WHAT DO YOU WANT?

"One half of knowing what you want is knowing what you must give up before you get it."

—Sidney Howard

"Life is not only knowing what you want but what you'll settle for."

—Joan Bennett Kennedy

Many people are frustrated, not because they don't have the ability to succeed, but because they have never figured out what they want. Blessed are those who have a clear vision and are willing to give up any distraction that gets in the way.

Do you know exactly what you want?

Do you have a good understanding of why you want it?

What are some good things in your life that are keeping you from pursuing the best things?

Have you ever pursued something with passion only to find that it wasn't what you thought it was?

How can someone learn to know what they want?

Do you know someone who is pursuing the wrong thing or the wrong person?

How can we grow to desire better things?

What to you need to start doing or stop doing to achieve your goals?

WHAT GIVES LIFE MEANING?

"Life is not primarily a quest for pleasure, as Freud believed, or a quest for power, as Alfred Adler taught, but a quest for meaning."

—Viktor Frankl

"The meaning of life is to find your gift. The purpose of life is to give it away."

—Pablo Picasso

The meaning of life is expressed through what you do based on the motive of why you do it. We can go to college, work endless hours, and make millions but still wake up to a life without meaning.

———————————————————

What gives your life meaning?

Is the meaning of life important to you, or are you content to "eat, drink, and be merry for tomorrow we will die"?

Was there a certain age when you began to consider the purpose of your life?

Are there some purpose-driven companies, non-profits, or NGO's where you would like to work?

Have you ever read Viktor Frankl's famous book *Man's Search for Meaning*?

If you were to die today, would you be content with what you've done with your life?

Is the purpose of your life based more on a "who" than a "what"?

WHAT IF?

"What if I fall? Oh, my darling, what if you fly?"

—Unknown

"What if...? A question we ask to hurt ourselves."

—Susan Fletcher

"What if" is the beginning question for all creative ideas and imagination. It is the premise for a possibility that has yet to come into existence. "What if there was a talking mouse named Mickey?" asked Walt Disney.

Do you value questions that begin with "What if?"

Can you think of some amazing discoveries that were the result of someone thinking outside the box?

Do some "what if" questions—like "What if we were billionaires?"—seem like a waste of time?

Can you think of three or four "what if" questions that might help you consider making an important change?

Do you believe you have a good imagination that allows you to consider and evaluate things that are not yet?

In his film *It's a Wonderful Life,* Capra asks: "What if you had never been born?" How would you answer this question?

Are you already too much of a dreamer, or would you benefit from some big "what if" thinking?

WHAT MOTIVATES YOU?

"Motivation is when your dreams put on work clothes."

—Benjamin Franklin

"I've got a dream that's worth more than my sleep."

—Unknown

A motive is a reason why. It's your reason to get out of bed, to sweat and suffer, and to make a sacrifice. Motivation comes easier when you've tried and succeeded. Even the tiniest victory can keep you going.

———————————————

Would you describe yourself as highly motivated?

What are some results that have caused you to believe your motivation will bring about the change you desire?

Have you ever lost motivation to continue doing something?

Is it common that people lose motivation because they are content with the status quo and don't want to take the risk of actually succeeding?

Have you ever been motivated by fear?

Have you ever been motivated by the cheers of a crowd or the words of a friend?

What is the wrong way to motivate you?

How can you become more motivated to do the things you need to do?

WINNING

"Winning isn't everything; it's the only thing."

—Vince Lombardi

"The determination to win is the better part of winning."

—Daisaku Ikeda

It's not wrong to want to win, but there are right and wrong ways to do it. Learning to be a good winner is harder than learning to be a gracious loser. Losing is naturally humbling, but winning comes with our natural tendency to gloat.

How important is winning?

Have you ever been guilty of excessive celebration after a win?

Are you so good at a game that you almost always win?

Is competition a regular part of your life?

How did you handle winning and losing as a child?

Is there a sport or game you refuse to play because you always lose?

Have you ever won a random prize, a raffle, or a lottery?

How can you be a better winner, a more gracious loser, or a healthy competitor?

WISDOM

"You don't receive wisdom; we must discover it for ourselves after a journey that no one can take for us or spare us."

—Marcel Proust

"Knowledge comes from learning. Wisdom comes from living."

—Anthony Douglas Williams

Wisdom is the crowning jewel of a virtuous life. It is the fruit that grows out of years of making hard decisions, making big mistakes, and struggling. Wisdom only comes with time, and it is a gift from God.

Who is someone you respect for their wisdom?

How have the challenges of life produced wisdom in you?

Have you ever been foolish?

What is the difference between knowledge and wisdom?

Are some people born with wisdom, or does it only come through hard knocks and experience?

Do you read books written by wise men and women?

Have you ever memorized any wise sayings that guide you in your life?

What is the wisest decision you've ever made?

How can you grow in wisdom and be the man or woman that others pursue for counsel?

WOMEN

"Women are the real architects of society."

—Harriet Beecher Stowe

"Women are the sustaining force of any society; they think of the children and the next generation's chances."

—Margo MacDonald

Women have had a rough go ever since the beginning. They took the rap for getting kicked out of the Garden. They've been treated like slaves, struggled in childbirth, and fought for the right to vote. Still, they shine.

———————————————

What is the best part of being a woman?

Who are the women you admire most?

What qualities make a woman a woman?

Do you believe it is harder to be a woman than a man?

Does the fight for equality with men ever seem to diminish the uniqueness of being a woman?

Are there things women just naturally do better?

Who are women from history we should study?

How can we celebrate women more and value their uniqueness?

WORDS YOU LOVE

"Words are, in my not-so-humble opinion, our most inexhaustible source of magic. Capable of both inflicting injury, and remedying it."
—Albus Dumbledore (J.K. Rowling)

"My favorite three words in the English language are 'I don't know,' because every time I say them, I learn something new."
—Timothy Leary

A logophile is a lover of words. And even though words can be clumsy, inadequate, and slow to come, they give us a fairly eloquent and precise vehicle for expressing ourselves. Words are what we have.

———————————————————

Are you good with words?

Do you have a favorite word?

How well did you perform on spelling tests, reading tests, and vocabulary tests?

Would you say your vocabulary is above average?

What do you think of people who use big words?

Is there an author whose use of words amazes you?

Have you ever found yourself at a loss for words?

What are some new words recently added to the dictionary?

How can you use your words more wisely?

WORKRY

"A day of worry is more exhausting than a day of work."

—John Lubbock

"Worry never robs tomorrow of its sorrow; it only saps today of its joy."

—Leo Buscaglia

Ironically, it is the fool who should learn to worry and the wise who should learn to stop. Worry is an expression of misguided love and concern. Worry is work and nothing to show for it.

Are you a worrier?

What are you worried about?

Was your mom or dad a worrier?

What is the most worried you have ever been in your life?

How can we take all the nervous energy produced by worry and put it to good use?

What is the silliest fear you've ever had?

Do you ever pray when you get worried?

Who do you call when you get worried?

How can you handle worry better?

CHRISTMAS

"I will honor Christmas in my heart, and try to keep it all the year."

—Ebenezer Scrooge (Charles Dickens)

"For it is in giving that we receive."

—Francis of Assisi

Christmas means so many different things to people all over the world. For Christians, the birth of Jesus is the source of all gifts, celebrations, family, and every good thing. Joy to the world!

What does Christmas mean to you?

How do you like to celebrate Christmas?

What was Christmas like for you family, and how did you celebrate when you were a child?

What was the best present you ever received for Christmas?

What was the best present you ever gave someone for Christmas?

Was there one Christmas you will never forget?

Are there some Christmas traditions you observe every year?

How can you make this Christmas especially memorable?

How can we remove holiday frenzy and get back to the real meaning of Christmas?

WORST EVER

"Dying is the worst thing that's ever happened to me."

—Ed Bloom

"Remember the tea kettle—it is always up to its neck in hot water, yet it sings!"

—Unknown

Life's worst moments can be quite memorable. Our "worsts" tend to produce our best stories. Unfortunately, the story doesn't come without some pain.

Do you see value in recalling your worst experiences?

Do you have a funny "worst"story (haircut, birthday, flight, relationship, vacation)?

What is the worst thing you've tasted?

What is the worst thing anyone has said to you?

What is the worst thing to ever come out of your mouth?

Do you have a worst day ever? A worst year ever?

Do you know someone who seems to be having the worst life ever?

What is the worst thing that's ever happened to you?

How do you comfort yourself after experiencing life's inevitable "worst things"?

Is it possible that our worsts are other people's "not bads"?

What's the worst thing I've ever done to you, and have you been able to forgive me?

YOUR AGE

"Don't let your age control your life. Let your life control your age."

—Anthony Douglas Williams

"Count your age by friends, not years. Count your life by smiles, not tears."

—John Lennon

You can say that age is just a state of mind, but tell that to the teenager waiting for a driver's permit or the couple too old to adopt. Your age matters.

———————————————————

Do you mind telling people how old you are?

When you were a child, did you anxiously wait to get to a certain age?

What do you think about having a required age for driving, marriage, military service, drinking, etc.?

Have you ever felt that you were being judged based on your age?

At what age would you consider someone to be old?

Do you believe there's a secret to staying young?

What is the best part of being your current age?

If you could live perpetually at any age, how old would you choose to be?

Does my age affect our relationship in any way?

YOUR COMFORT ZONE

"Comfort zones are where dreams go to die."
—Russell Brunson

"The only thing that is stopping you from where you are to where you want to go is your comfort zone."
—Dhaval Gaudier

The problem with comfort zones is they disguise themselves as success. We fool ourselves, thinking the absence of struggle and pain are the endgame.

How would you describe your comfort zone?

In what ways are you living outside your comfort zone right now?

Was there a season in your life where you were especially successful in living outside your comfort zone?

What is one thing you were able to accomplish by leaving your comfort behind?

Who were the people in your life that challenged you to go beyond your comfort zone to accomplish something?

What is one area of your life that needs to be challenged right now?

What motivates you to live outside your comfort zone?

Is it discouraging to think that life is merely a never-ending decision to live outside your comfort zone?

How can I encourage you to leave your comfort zone?

YOUR NAME

"A name represents identity, a deep feeling, and holds tremendous significance to its owner."
—Rachel Ingber

"If you build a good name, eventually, that name will be its own currency."
—William S. Burroughs

The sweetest word in any language is someone's name. Names can have honor or be tarnished. Names have meaning, and usually come with a story.

Do you know what your name means?

Why did your parents choose the name you were given?

Have you ever wanted to change your name?

If you were to change your name, what would be some of your favorite options?

What is your middle name?

Do you believe that the meaning of our name influences who we are and how we live?

Did anyone in your family talk about protecting or guarding the integrity of the family name?

Do you know where you last name comes from and what it means?

What do you think about a woman changing her name when she gets married?

What names do you want to give your children?

YOUR PASSION

"Nothing great in the world has ever been accomplished without passion."
—Georg Wilhelm Friedrich Hegel

"To practice any art, no matter how well or badly, is a way to make your soul grow. So do it."
—Kurt Vonnegut

To have passion is to have a powerful, compelling emotion for something. Some say passion is the only path to success. Others say passion is overrated.

Do you believe passion is overrated?

Is there someone in your life whose passion you admire?

What is something you once had passion for but no longer do?

Do you have a passion for a product or brand?

Can passion be conjured up, cultivated, or fabricated?

What are you most passionate about right now?

Do you have passion to create something or achieve something?

Have you built personal relationships on a shared passion?

Do you have a passion for something or someone that is irrational?

Has your passion for something ever been destructive?

Is it important for a husband and wife to share similar passions?

TURNING POINTS

"The turning point in the life of those who succeed usually comes at the moment of some crisis."

—Napolean Hill

"Commitment is that turning point in your life when you seize the moment to alter your destiny."

—Denis Waitley

Turning points are dynamic moments in a story when everything changes. Life as we know it will never be the same. Our story is now moving in a new direction.

What would you say are some of life's big turning points?

How does life impose turning points without asking permission?

Did you experience a major turning point in your life as a child?

Is there a turning point in your life that was the direct result of your decision to make it happen?

What was the happiest turning point in your life? The saddest? The hardest?

Do you feel that there is a need for a turning point in your life right now?

What is a turning point you're looking forward to?

If you could make a turning point happen for someone you love, what would it be?

What have been some turning points in our relationship?

"WE LONG TO BE
DEEPLY KNOWN
AND, IN SPITE OF IT,
TO FIND OURSELVES
STILL DEEPLY LOVED."

—Curt Wilkinson

Index

blueparkbooks.com

Made in the USA
Columbia, SC
19 February 2023

12307068R00248